The Best Strategy & War Games

Strategies & Secrets™

BY COMPUTER GAMES STRATEGY PLUS

SAN FRANCISCO · PARIS · DÜSSELDORF · SOEST

Associate Publisher	GARY MASTERS
Acquisitions Manager	KRISTINE PLACHY
Developmental Editor and Copy Editor	TERRENCE O'DONNELL
Project Editor	MAUREEN ADAMS
Production Coordination	LABRECQUE PUBLISHING SERVICES
Book Design and Production	WILLIAM SALIT DESIGN
Proofreader	RACHEL FUDGE
Cover Designer	ARCHER DESIGN

Library of Congress Card Number: 96-70734
ISBN: 0-7821-2026-1

Manufactured in the United States of America

10 9 8 7 6 5 4 3 2

TABLE OF CONTENTS

INTRODUCTION

The Best Strategy & War Games is a treasure chest for computer gamers. This combination book/CD/magazine subscription, specifically devoted to PC strategy and war gamers, is one of the best buys on the market today.

THE SUBSCRIPTION

This book/CD package includes a six-issue subscription to COMPUTER GAMES Strategy Plus magazine. Send no money—your subscription is already paid. To activate your subscription, simply tear out the form at the back of the book, fill it out, fold, seal, put a stamp on it, and mail it. (If you're already a subscriber, your subscription will be extended by six issues.)

If the subscription proof-of-purchase form is missing from this book, send a photocopy of the book cover along with your sales receipt to COMPUTER GAMES Strategy Plus, P.O. Box 3000, Denville, NJ 07834.

THE BOOK

This book is packed with hints, tips, and strategies for playing computer war games—all written by some of the world's leading reviewers and players of strategy and war game products. These battle-scarred veterans have braved hundreds of enemy attacks to discover the secrets of the games so you may live where others have died. In this collection, they share with you the important tips; successful, and some unsuccessful, strategies and tactics; and, in desperate situations, the cheats necessary to provide you with the essential ammunition you need for V-I-C-T-O-R-Y, no matter what your choice of war game may be.

The chapters in this book cover today's most popular, best-selling, and challenging war games. Whether you want to colonize, expand, and dominate the world in MicroProse's *Civilization II*; relive key North-South conflicts in TalonSoft's *Battleground*: Gettysburg, Shiloh, or Waterloo; or enhance your war efforts with the magic and sorcery dimension in New World Computing's *Heroes of Might and Magic*, you can get all of the valuable gaming information you need in this book.

Before you dive into specific games, though, take a look at the first chapter, "On War," which is a compilation of general strategies of warfare—both from defensive and offensive perspectives. The insights in this chapter come from not just war game veterans, but from real war veterans. Information on air defense tactics, penetrating the other guy's air defense systems, achieving air superiority over enemies, dealing with mine fields, and the pros and cons of deceit are among the many real war strategies you'll find in this chapter to prepare you fully for battle in the computer war game environment.

The balance of *The Best Strategy & War Games* presents a liberal arrangement of war games, from those with more traditional theaters of war to those that add elements of high-tech weaponry or fantasy (or both). After studying the general tactics of war in Chapter 1, and the specific hints and tips in the chapters covering your favorite games, you will have all the intelligence information you need to carry out your missions and conquer your on-screen enemies.

THE CD-ROM

The CD-ROM at the back of this book includes demos of all but one of the games presented in this book as well as some other goodies, such as a video interview with MicroPose's *Civilization II* designer Brian Reynolds. You'll find hours of entertainment with these playable demos. There's nothing like seeing if you'll really like a game, before you plunk down $50 or $60 for it. (Now that's real reconnaissance!) After you've mastered one of your favorite war games, check out the CD and install a demo for another game that you always wanted to try out, like *Caesar II* by Impressions, Interplay's *Command & Conquer*, Blizzard Entertainment's *Warcraft II*, or . . .

ACKNOWLEDGMENTS

The editors at Sybex would like to extend a special thanks to the editors, contributors, and staff at COMPUTER GAMES Strategy Plus, in particular: Yale Brozen, Publisher; Steve Bauman, Managing Editor; and Scott Udell, Associate Editor. Steve and Scott were instrumental in providing Sybex with all the elements you see in this collection, including not only the articles and screen shots, but much-appreciated guidance in organizing the content into an excellent strategy guide covering a variety of products. Special thanks also goes to Alan Brush, Circulation Director, who was helpful in providing the means for you, the reader, to extend your gaming enjoyment beyond this book and subscribe to future issues of COMPUTER GAMES Strategy Plus.

The writers who contributed articles to this book, are noted professionals in their field. In alphabetical order, they are: Joe Grant Bell, Michael Bowen, M. Evan Brooks,

Chuck Klimushyn, Jeff Lackey, Eric Leaf, Robert Mayer, Michael K. Robel, Phil The, Scott Udell, Cindy Vanous, and Mark H. Walker.

This book would not have been possible without Gary Masters, Associate Publisher at Sybex, whose inspiration, support, and enthusiasm of all things game started this project rolling; Terry O'Donnell, who sweat bullets to pull together the articles and art and develop the book on a deadly schedule; and Peter Kuhns and Maureen Adams for additional editorial support.

Finally, thank you to at Labrecque Publishing Services, in particular, Tory McLearn, who managed the book's production; and William Salit, the book's designer who produced these pages.

1

On War

Before you grab that joystick and get ready to rock 'n' roll through the war games covered in this book, you might want to prep your effort with a good look at this chapter. Here several veteran war gamers devoted their collective wisdom on various aspects to strategic command of your forces, both offensively and defensively. So lock and load, and use these pointers to shape your own game plan in your favorite war game.

AIR DEFENSE

This section on air defense will discuss the purpose, deployment, and counters for you air defense forces. Air defense forces have two main purposes. The first is to protect the ground force or its air fields. The second, and much harder purpose, is to provide defensive air superiority over the friendly force's airfields by denying the enemy air force the ability to operate in friendly airspace. The first purpose is more or less successfully conducted by most forces, while the second almost never is. One example of this is the 1973 Arab-Israeli War, where the Egyptian Air Defense network kept the Israeli Air Force out of the battle until a gap could be opened.

There are two types of defense: *point* and *area*. Point defense is used to protect airfields and other high value targets, such as command and control headquarters. Area defense protects larger targets such as deployed ground forces or cities. While existing air defense networks can adequately protect deployed ground forces, they still cannot adequately protect a target such as a city. As was seen in the Gulf War, even a successful intercept of an incoming missile or aircraft can cause damage to a city as the wreckage plummets to the ground, even though the warhead was destroyed.

Ground units provide limited self-defense with their machine guns and automatic cannon. For more effective defense, air defense platoons are usually placed in direct support of a battalion. These may consist of Vulcan-Stinger teams, Bradley Stinger Fighting Vehicles, or Avengers. In each case, these weapons include a gun and a missile. The BSFV and Avenger can fire mounted, but the Stinger gunner must dismount from the Vulcan to use his missile. Eventually, BSFV will replace the Vulcans in mechanized units. There is usually a general support platoon of Stingers that supplements the gun-missile platoons. Stingers are also used for self-defense of HAWK and Patriot batteries.

Improved HAWKs and Patriots provide a more extended air defense envelope that covers a very large area. The Patriot also provides a Anti-Tactical Ballistic Missile

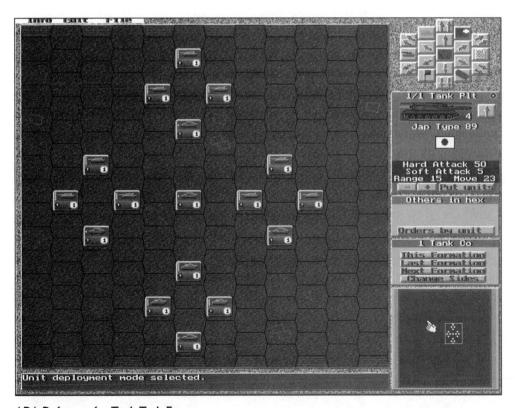

ADA Defense of a Tank Task Force

defense, but it was originally designed to be used against aircraft. These systems will be supplemented by the Theater High Altitude Air Defense System (THAAD) and the Corps Surface to Air Missile (CORPSAM).

These weapons provide overlapping coverage of the battlefield, both in altitude and range.

The Stinger has a range of 16 hexes. It can either accompany the forces forward, which with Avengers or Vulcans is a *bad thing* because they don't enjoy protection equal to the other vehicles, and their distinctive appearance makes them a sure target. In this case, they should leap frog forward from vantage point to vantage point, providing continuous coverage with bounding overwatch.

When protecting a force, remember that high performance aircraft (jets) usually use valleys as avenues of approach, while rotary wing aircraft use ridges. In either event, the weapons can be sighted to provide aerial kill zones.

Next consider how to protect an area of operations at the level of a theater commander using *Harpoon II*. While most *Harpoon* scenarios are challenging, none have shown a full ADA belt. This figure shows the general layout.

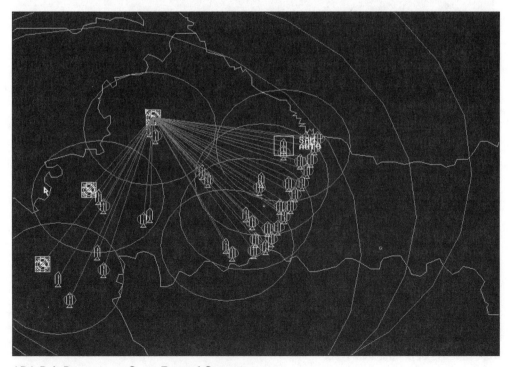

ADA Belt Protecting a Corps Zone of Operations

Up forward are the Stingers protecting the forces along the Forward Line of Troops (FLOT). Notice the two up and one back configuration as the ADA platoons protect the forward and reserve forces in each brigade. Omitted here are additional Stinger units protecting trains and command posts. Also omitted is the curtain of fire that the front line troops can put with machine guns and automatic cannon. The Stinger is essentially a self-defense weapon used only when ground troops are directly threatened by aircraft or helicopters.

Next, deploy ADA units to protect your friendly air bases and some command and control facilities with HAWK missile batteries. Third, deploy a HAWK belt across your entire front to protect the ground force. Note that each battery's fire overlaps with its neighbor's on the left and right. Each battery is placed approximately one-half to one-third of its range back from the FLOT in order to engage enemy forces across it. HAWK will eventually be replaced by CORPSAM.

Finally, PATRIOT batteries are placed, again one third of their range back, to provide an additional layer of protection. Each Hawk and Patriot battery may well have Stingers for self-defense. Patriot, of course, also provides some tactical ballistic missile protection and has been considerably upgraded since the Gulf War.

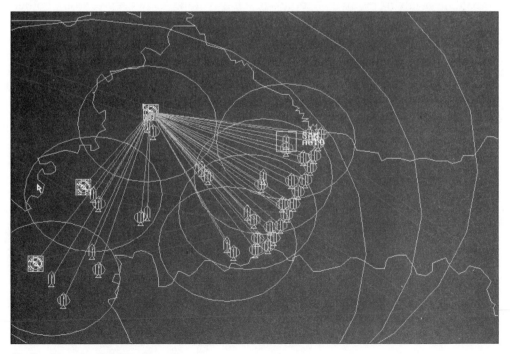

Air Corridors for Friendly Aircraft

You also need to provide your aircraft corridors to enter and exit friendly air space.

Games do not normally model these corridors, but players could use Navzones for this purpose. These provide routes in friendly air defense zones through which friendly aircraft may fly on their way to or from missions.

Finally, you must set up warning and engagement criteria to avoid shooting at your own aircraft. Air Defense Warnings are: Red, Enemy Air Attack Imminent; Yellow, Enemy Air Attack Possible; or White, Enemy Air Attack not Likely. Control Statues are: Weapons Free, ADA units may fire at any aircraft; Weapons Tight, ADA units may fire at enemy aircraft positively identified as hostile; or Weapons Hold, ADA units may fire only at enemy aircraft engaging friendly units or in self defense. Self defense is never prohibited. For the Gulf War, the U.S. predominantly operated in a Status of White-Hold. Weapons status for weapons guarding a corridor is almost always weapons tight because you don't want to shoot down friendly aircraft leaving or coming back to your side of the battlefield. Conversely, any aircraft outside of a corridor may be fair game for the *duckhunters*.

This layered protection means that any enemy force must first neutralize the local air defense forces of the frontline units. (Actually, these units seldom attack enemy aircraft merely flying by, on the grounds that if they don't bother us, we won't bother them and will avoid attracting attention.) Then the Hawk Batteries, as well as the Patriot Belt, must be isolated and destroyed. Finally, if your goal is to attack command and control facilities or airfields, then these forces, too, must be destroyed. It is a daunting task and one that requires a lot of coordination.

THE OTHER GUYS

Now let's explore the niceties of the Other Guy's Air Defense Belt. Here we'll use the former Soviet Union as the model for the Opposing Force (OPFOR).

Because the OPFOR is very concerned about your Air Force's ability to conduct the air-to-ground support of your ground forces and also nearly paranoid about maintaining an inviolability of its own air space, its ground forces have a very heavy air defense structure. Each motorized rifle company has three SA-7 (or equivalent) SAMs. Each Motorized Rifle Regiment has an Air Defense Battery with 4 ZSU-23-4 AAA guns and four SA-9s. At Division, there is an ADA battalion, with five batteries of SA-6s or SA-8s. At the Corps or Army level, there is usually a battalion of SA-11s, and at the Front, a Brigade of SA-12s. To summarize, one Motorized Rifle's ADA assets and supporting slice looks like the figure on the following page.

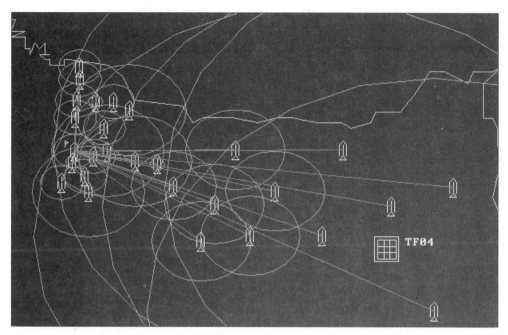

Other Guy Air Defense Belt

ADA ASSETS AND SUPPORTING SLICE	
ADA SYSTEM	**NUMBER**
SA-7's	81
ZSU-23-4	12
SA-9	12
SA-8	16
SA-11	6
SA-12	6
Total Systems	129

As you can see in the previous table, this is quite an impressive array. The table does not show nearly the amount of SA-7s available to the division, and for simplicity, only one division and its fair share of other ADA systems is shown.

You can readily see the layered defense of the enemy belt. Note that just like the U.S. belt, it provides for overlapping fire for each ADA unit, to reduce the consequences

> ### N O T E
> In this list the French Croatale Missile was substituted for the SA-11s and SA-7s were substituted for the SA-9s because *Harpoon II* does not currently model these SAMs.

of the loss of any one missile unit. The units are also layered in depth, much more so than the U.S. belts, in order to present a much more difficult approach to the target for attacking aircraft. Each layer of the belt overlaps both with its own neighbors and its higher and lower counterparts.

Each missile belt overlaps in altitude as well. If it were possible to turn the *Harpoon II* display on its side and look at it from ground level, you would see bubbles much like those shown in the figure below. This ensures that no aircraft can ingress or egress from its target unmolested by ADA fire.

The Front (equivalent to a U.S. Army) also controls aircraft. In this case, they have been allotted 12 each MiG-29s, MiG-27s, SU-25s, and SU-27s. Eighteen F-16s, 18 F-15Cs, 18 F-15Es, 6 F-117s, and 18 AH-64 were also added to the U.S. side—representing a slice of aircraft that may be available to a corps or JTF commander—and a solitary Aegis Class Cruiser.

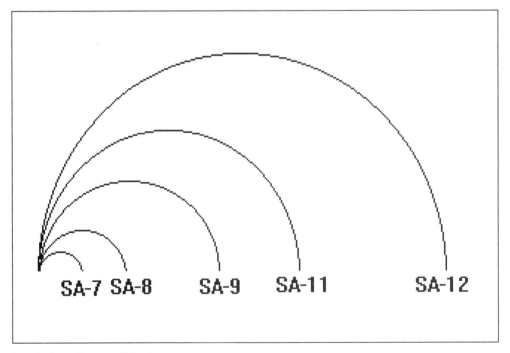

Interlocking Fires at Altitude

Air Superiority

In order for ground forces to maneuver freely on the ground, one side or the other must have air superiority. There are a number of methods by which this can be accomplished.

- **Defensive Counter-Air**: This is the sort of battle made famous by the Battle of Britain. The British did not really have the ability to go hit the German air fields, and were reduced to fighting the *Luftwaffe* over England. While the British were successful, destroying enemy fighters in the air is the least effective way of gaining air superiority, because you stand to lose a lot of your own fighters.

- **Offensive Counter-Air**: This entails attacking the enemy's air bases in the hope of destroying a large part, if not all, of his air force on the ground. The Israelis accomplished this successfully during the Six Days' war. They had a relatively easy time of it because the Egyptian Air Defense Belt was not particularly strong and they timed the attack well.

In Viet Nam, the U.S. had uncontested air superiority over the south, but in the North they had a difficult time because rules of engagement prevented forces from actively attacking many of the SAM sites, which were inflicting relatively heavy casualties on U.S. planes. In Iraq, the U.S. corrected this problem by first suppressing the Iraqi ADA system so that their planes could fly more or less freely over the battlefield.

The first step in gaining air superiority against an enemy with a sophisticated ADA defense system is to destroy the ability of that system to influence the battle. This is also true for ground units when they request air support. First, the ADA threat needs to be suppressed or eliminated. In Iraq the U.S. used a variety of methods of suppressing the ADA threat. Army systems were integral to this effort. The Army Tactical Missile System (ATACMS) was used to obliterate an enemy ADA battery deep inside Iraq in order to open a corridor for B-52 strikes. Apache helicopters also successfully attacked enemy ADA units to open corridors. More conventional methods of SAM suppression were also flown by Wild Weasel aircraft, which specialize in hunting down SAM radars, and F-117s to take out critical command and control nodes.

Not to be overlooked is the value of artillery in taking out those pesky frontline air defense systems, the SA-7 and ZSU-23-4. Occasionally even direct-fire systems (tanks and Bradleys) can get into the act if the enemy ADA systems are foolish enough to show themselves. Since they are radically different in appearance from most other battlefield systems, they draw fire like honey does bees. Ground forces can also open gaps by rampaging through the enemy rear and destroying ADA batteries, as the Israelis were able to do in 1973 after crossing the canal. That act finally let the IAF, which had been suffering terrible losses trying to help the ground forces, into the fray again.

TAKE DOWN!

Now, the whole purpose of the take-down of the ADA belt is to destroy the enemy's ability to deny friendly aircraft the use of the sky. In that way, SAMs are much like submarines. They can deny use of an area, but they can't really control it.

There are two different situations in which an attacker will want to suppress or take down an air defense network. The first is when either fixed or rotary wing aircraft are providing support to ground troops, either individually or together. The second is when fixed-wing aircraft are trying to penetrate to targets deep in the enemy rear.

Suppression of Enemy Air Defense

In the first case this operation, called Suppression of Enemy Air Defense (SEAD), is accomplished by a combination of direct and indirect fire. Frontline units, knowing they are going to get air support, can change their engagement priority and attack air defense systems to increase the airplanes' survivability. Indirect fire, either with area or precision weapons, can also do the job. The many SA-7s or their equivalent (carried in the BMPs) have to be fired from the open. Therefore, the gunners may be neutralized by an air-burst artillery barrage. The main targets to hit in this case are the ZSU-23-4s and the SA-6 carriers that are present in the regimental area.

When army helicopters and Air Force CAS work together in a joint attack, the helicopters may be assigned the job of suppressing the ADA targets, while the jets work over the tanks and BMPs. SEAD is somewhat complicated, because normally friendly artillery fire is *turned off* over the flight paths of the incoming airplanes, to avoid the possibility of hitting them.

This operation is a difficult task to properly synchronize, but can pay large dividends when done properly. When playing with air missions in *Tanks*, you should remember to target ADA weapons early to destroy their protective, interlocking umbrella over the enemy force. In the game, air strikes occur before ground movement, so you have to keep the suppression in mind at all times.

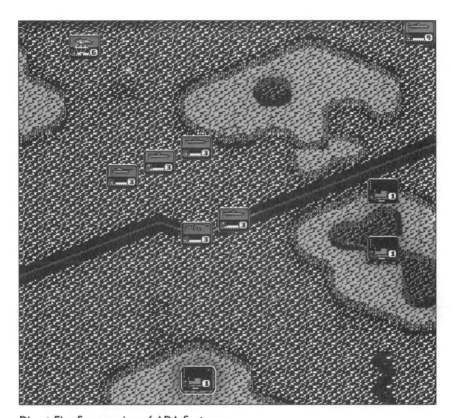

Direct Fire Suppression of ADA Systems

Since there is not really any way to tell which BMP has the SA-7, it is harder to suppress SA-7s. However, these gunners, like their American counterparts, probably don't wish to call attention to themselves by attacking aircraft that is not already targeting them.

In deeper penetrations, there are different methods to be used. First, the frontline systems may be left alone, again because these are self-defense weapons, and will normally only engage the enemy in certain circumstances. If it is necessary to suppress these systems, it will usually be accomplished by artillery or battlefield rockets. Occasionally, Army helicopters may attack to assist the penetration effort. Both these methods were used during Desert Storm. The 1st Infantry Division fired an Army Tactical Missile System to obliterate one ADA battery, while Apaches from the 101st Airborne Division attacked another to clear a path for Air Force aircraft.

This attack is much like conducting a penetration attack. It is nothing fancy, just destroy enough systems to open a gap for your planes to fly through. Occasionally, an

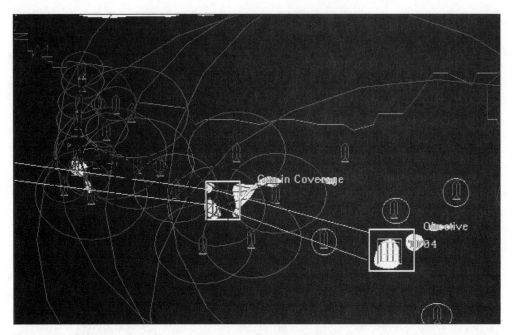

Penetration Plan

open flank can be found to assist the strike in penetrating. Remember, if you will, the use of a mountain chain leading from Iran to Iraq to allow Tomahawk cruise missiles to penetrate the Iraqi air defense as well as have a navigation fix. The Israeli aircraft in the 1967 war also circled far out to sea to avoid enemy radar and to attack from an unexpected direction.

Executing SEAD in *Harpoon II*

Since *Harpoon II* does not model SSMs or Army artillery, you won't be able to use them. So in this case you'd have to use Apache gunships and Tomahawk cruise missiles to take out the lead systems. Your objective is to destroy the enemy airfield (the white rectangle marked "objective" in the figure above). For your purposes the enemy airfield holds the Front Command and Control systems as well as the majority of the Front's supporting aircraft. As you study the network, you see that there are naturally open flanks which we could use to the north, but the Rules of Engagement prohibit us from overflying that country. Fortunately, a found gap in the ADA belt can be exploited by attacking only a single site instead of multiple ones.

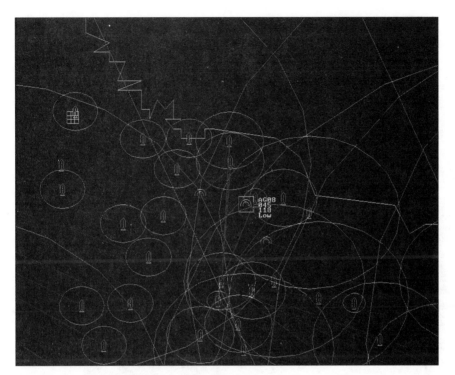

AG08
045
118
Low

Apaches Attacking to Make Initial Penetration

Because you wish to minimize pilot exposure, attack the forward ADA sites with Apache Gunships and the deeper ADA sites with Tomahawks from your supporting cruiser. Now, you could attack the target with just the cruise missiles, but they are an easy target for an alerted enemy with advanced fighters and warning.

Here is your plan of attack: First, Apaches will attack the sites enclosed in the green rectangle. This opens the initial gap for the Air Force planes to fly through. Second, the cruiser will attack the enemy sites enclosed in white circles; and finally, the Air Force will have to fight through, attacking the targets marked with blue rectangles before they can attack the airbase.

The cruiser *Antietam* fires four cruise missiles at the SAM sites defending the airfield while Apache helicopters attack the SAM sites in the enemy front line and as deep as the division rear. As you can see, the initial attacks were successful.

The next phase is to begin taking out the batteries deeper in the enemy defensive belt. First send in F-117 stealth fighters to take out the batteries you want to eliminate.

Unfortunately, nearly all the Nighthawks were shot down without doing much damage in the example shown here. Apparently the overlapping fields of fire and radar coverage in the midst of the ADA belt could defeat even the stealth fighters, so F-15E Strike Eagles were used to take down the northern flank coverage and open the route to the target. As you can see in the following three figures, this was ultimately successful, as the airfield was destroyed.

The next lesson you can learn here is to ensure that you plot the strike's return courses before *Harpoon II*'s AI orders the planes to land, because they will take the shortest route

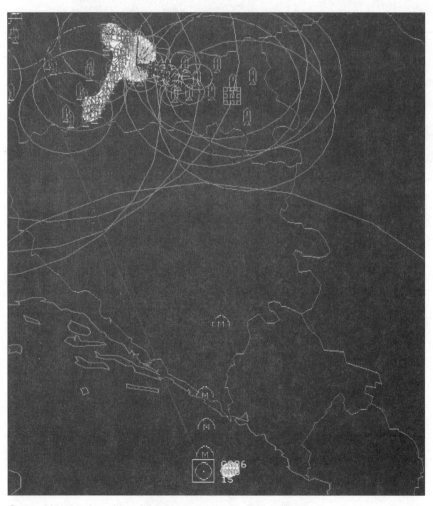

Cruise Missiles Attacking ADA Batteries in the Enemy Rear

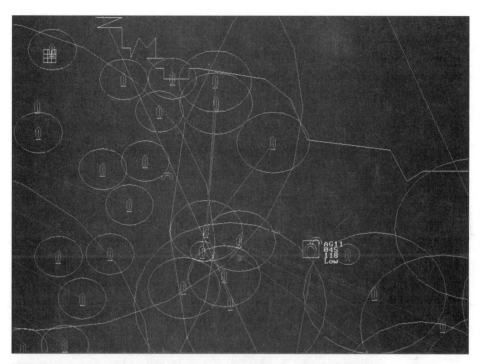

No plan survives contact with the enemy: switching to the north flank.

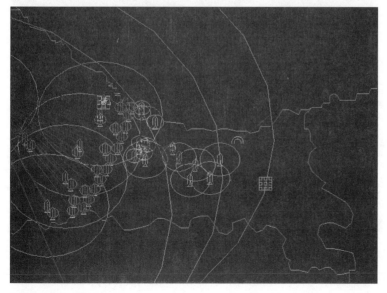

The path is open.

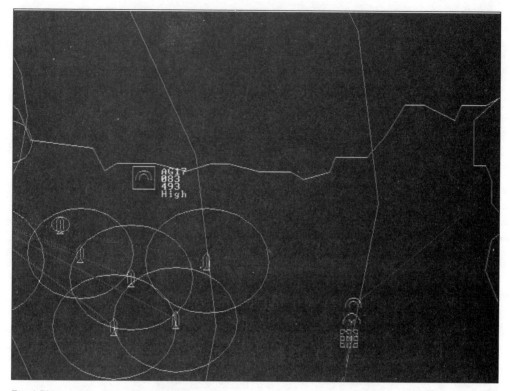

AG17
083
493
High

Final Phase: Attacking the Airfield

back to their home airfield. In this case, failing to do so meant having return flights over-flying the intact sections of the enemy air defense belt; of course, several were lost.

THE AGONY OF DECEIT!

In this section let's turn to the role of deceit on the battlefield. Deception relates squarely to the principles of surprise and security. Surprise merely means trying to attack from an unanticipated direction or method, while security mainly focuses on preventing yourself from being surprised or keeping your plans from the enemy.

Computer intelligences are immune to deceit, because they only do what they're programmed to do, or they cheat. While playing a game where the computer can see all your units and moves as you make them, it is difficult to deceive the silicon opponent.

Nonetheless, it can be done. The computer can't read your mind, even if it can know your moves and possible moves—remember that. In any event, hiding your true intentions from your enemy is always worthwhile.

One goal of deceit is to force the enemy to hold his forces in their present location, to allow you a free hand elsewhere. The perfect example of this is the deception which resulted in Hitler's forbidding any movement of his troops toward Normandy (because he thought the threat of an attack in the Pas de Calais was overwhelming). The threat of an amphibious assault froze Iraqi units in place on the coast. Similarly, deployment and activity in the Wadi al Batin made the Iraqis continue to look there for an attack.

One of the earliest methods of deceit was to place cavalry in front of a deploying force to screen or cover its movements from the watching enemy. The cavalry, being taller than the infantry behind it, blocked the enemy's line of sight. Consequently, the enemy had no way of telling how the opposite force was setting up until the cavalry went off to the flanks and uncovered the infantry force, now ready for battle. Naturally, this only worked if the ground was relatively flat (as most battlefields were in antiquity), because if the enemy occupied a hill then the commanders could watch the deployment. The Coalition used screening techniques in the Gulf War as well. They used the Air Force in the cavalry role, to deprive the Iraqis of their ability to watch the Coalition Force deploy and shift for the great end-around.

Today, armored cavalry regiments cover an army corps' deployment. The cavalry attacks (or defends) and seeks to strip off enemy reconnaissance elements and, if possible, penetrate into the enemy main defensive belts. The farther they can get, the longer the corps commander can delay exposing his main effort. When defending, cavalry attempts to force the enemy to deploy his main body, telegraphing the main effort to the corps commander.

How can you deceive your opponent in a game? Well, in this figure you can see army corps lined up for what looks to be an obvious penetration attack. Since in most games (board and computer) you get a helicopter's-eye view of the battlefield, this is what your opponent sees.

From what the enemy sees, he divines you intend to attack on the right. Accordingly, he places his armor division in reserve opposite your intended breach zone. This next figure shows your real plan. You'll use your mobility to race to the flank while your deception attack freezes his reserve in place for destruction. VII Corps did this during the Gulf War.

Okay, now you have played the same opponent several times and he's onto your wily ways. So this time, hold the starting line-up and actually conduct the attack as it

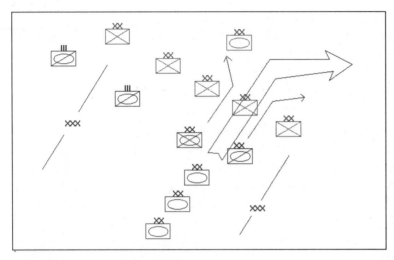

Is this what you are going to do?

looks, but delay the movement of the armor divisions for a turn or two. Your opponent may hold his reserve in place, expecting to see it appear over on the left flank. Once your forward divisions have penetrated his line, send the armor divisions through the gap, catching him flatfooted.

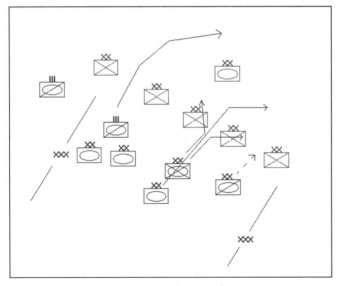

Or is it this?

Another way of deceiving the enemy is to threaten multiple areas simultaneously. While not really a deceitful act in itself, it does cast doubt upon the enemy about your intentions. Since he does not know which way you may strike, he may freeze.

This leads to opportunity. Because the best-laid plans of mice and men often go awry, you must be prepared to take advantage of an opportunity. For example, if the enemy detects your deception and reacts accordingly against your main effort, then you can merely turn your main effort into a supporting attack.

This principle also has a lesson: don't reinforce failure. If you have only a small reserve, commit it where you are being successful. Give ground, accept losses, do whatever you have to do in order to keep the enemy coming so you can strike him from an unanticipated direction.

These techniques work best in a double-blind environment, where your enemy can't see what you are doing, but can also work with perfect intelligence of your apparent plans. Remember, the target of the deception is not the force on the battlefield, but the mind of the enemy commander.

Let Him Go By, and Shoot Him in the Back

Another way to deceive the enemy is by using decoys or dummy positions. Many manual board games include dummy markers to increase the fog of war in what is otherwise a fairly open environment. The figure below shows one method of using decoys. In this example, the terrain supports two methods of firing on an attacking enemy. The positions in the South are where a force may be expected to defend. The commander has set up dummy tanks to lend credence to this story. However, what he is really doing is taking advantage of the hills and forests to break up the attacking enemy and separate the follow-on forces. The defense actually occupies the battle positions in the North. It seeks to take advantage of the limited visibility and increased vulnerability of the flanks and rear, to surprise the enemy and destroy him before he has a chance to respond.

This will probably only work once on any given piece of terrain, so a rehearsed escape route is a necessity. Needless to say, this takes quite a bit of nerve in either the field or on the game board, and the commander must be prepared to abandon his plan if he is discovered prematurely.

In the following figure, the blue tanks represent the actual positions of vehicles while the purple ones are decoys. The fine black lines show the actual fields of fire; the purple ones represent the decoy fields of fire. The light green object at the top is a scatterable minefield to slow or stop the next echelon from entering the kill zone, while the infantry platoon keeps that gap sealed. The minefield is fired only when the enemy enters the kill zone. Near the center, from left to right, are an anti-tank minefield, a road crater, and anti-tank ditch designed to turn the enemy to make him present his more vulnerable sides to our fire. Notice how the obstacles work for both battle positions.

A motorized rifle company is in the kill zone, although you would wait until a battalion is in the trap before you engage. The enemy enters in column, compressed by the hills and forest, and then spreads out for the assault on my decoy positions. Ideally, time the engagement to hit when he is just starting to deploy to platoon columns. Placing a tank section and an infantry squad in the decoy positions reinforces the deception and can assist in my escape.

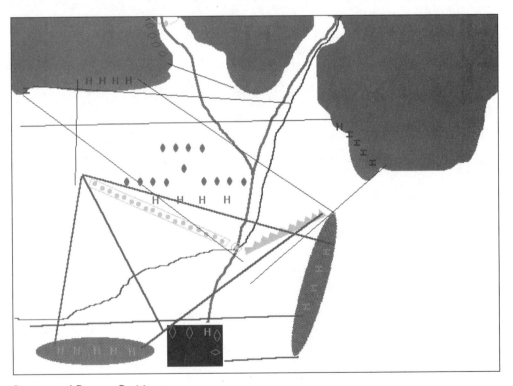

Decoys and Dummy Positions

MINEFIELDS: GETTING AROUND THE HARD SPOTS

In this section let's examine the use of minefields and other obstacles (and how to get around them). Minefields, ditches, wire, and other obstacles seek to do one of two things. The first is to deny the enemy access to a particular area. Examples of using obstacles to deny the enemy access to an area are as simple as the ditch around a Roman Legion's Encampment or as complex as the Maginot Line. The other purpose is to force or hold the enemy in a killing zone so you can destroy more of his systems. In either case, if you do not cover the obstacle with direct fire, it is only of limited value, because the enemy will be able to work his way through with only a little effort.

Minefields typically have a relatively low density and also have a low individual probability of kill per mine, less than five percent. However, even one vehicle finding a mine is enough to make everybody freeze. Most games do not allow the player to emplace obstacles other than minefields. Other obstacles are wire obstacles, ditches, log cribs, abitis, road craters, and bridge demolition, to name only a few.

Obstacle Course

Obstacles have two or three purposes. They can turn the enemy to make him move into a kill zone, present a flank, or hold him at a certain range so you have more time to kill him. They can also keep him out of a particular area.

If your game has Field Artillery Scatterable Minefields in it (and most don't, except Army simulations) a particular nasty trick is to dump them on the enemy right before he has breached your obstacle. This technique will definitely make the enemy's day more difficult.

Another use for them is to place them on your own gaps in your minefield to prevent the enemy from using them. The figure on the following page shows a series of minefields emplaced to do two things. The minefields on the flanks force the enemy into the kill zone for the lone tank platoon. The center minefield holds the enemy at the 50-percent probability of hit/kill range for the tank platoon. The tank platoon is able to fire on all the obstacles in order to keep the enemy from breaching them.

Air-dropped and ground-emplaced scatterable mine systems are also available. FASCAM also has other devious uses, but there is only a limited amount of the round

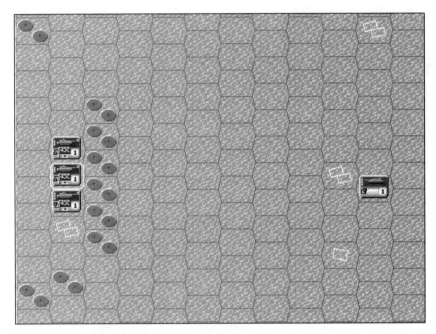

Typical Obstacle Employment

available and usually a brigade commander must authorize its use. A redeeming feature of FASCAM is that it has a self-destruct setting that prevents the friendly force from having to breach it. The self-destruct feature makes clearing obstacles after the war a little easier.

Obstacles must be tied in with natural terrain in order to be most effective. An easily bypassed obstacle is no good at all. In this next figure you see the effects of tying in obstacles with other terrain features. Note that the minefields are tied into hills or tree stands. On the northern flank, one of the minefields seals off an avenue of approach to prevent or slow an enemy flanking unit.

Other principles of obstacle employment emphasize integrating them into the scheme of maneuver, covering them with direct fire, and using them in depth.

Surprise is a very important aspect of emplacing obstacles that neither *Tanks* nor *Armored Fist* support. In both of these games, obstacles show up on the board when the game starts. To be realistic, they should only appear on the game board after the player discovers them, either through observation or by running into one of the mines.

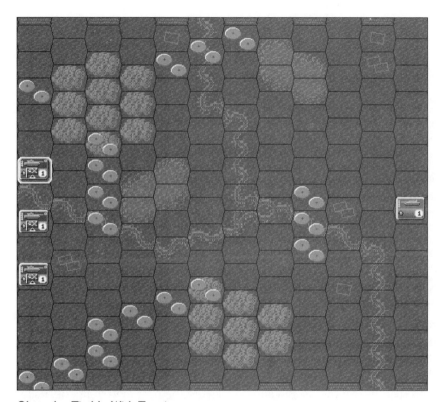

Obstacles Tied In With Terrain

Breach Maneuvers

Now that we have discussed how to emplace an obstacle, let's talk about how to breach it. First, remember that it is normally preferable to go around and find a bypass than it is to breach an obstacle. However, the ever-crafty enemy may want you to bypass the obstacle and construct his killing zone around the bypass that you find. In that case, you may have been better off to breach the obstacle in the first place. For this discussion, let's look at a decision to breach the obstacle, having failed to find a bypass.

Breaching is very simple in theory, but difficult in practice. It has but three steps:

★ First, secure the near side of the obstacle and place direct fire on it.

★ Second, suppress the far side by placing artillery, mortar, or direct fire on known or suspected enemy positions that can fire on the breach site.

★ Third, breach the obstacle.

Finally, upon completion secure the far side by moving through the breach.

After the above steps have been taken, continue the mission. You may have to go and chase the enemy out of his trenchworks or field fortifications.

Here is how to make it happen on a small scale in *Tanks* or *Armored Fist*. The first choice to make is whether or not you want to bypass, force, or breach the obstacle. Bypass is simple and usually the preferred course of action. Find a way around the obstacle. This has an inherent difficulty, because the enemy may leave the bypass open as a route into his real kill zone. The obvious bypass may also have an obstacle in it. The classic example of this is mining a ford next to a blown bridge.

Forcing, also known as bulling through, the obstacle means you just dive over it. The theory behind this concept is that the speed of the operation will limit the number of casualties you might take as compared to one of the other methods of getting through an obstacle. The Russians typically used this technique in World War II.

Theory Put to the Test

In game turns, here is how to breach a minefield. First, designate one unit (counter) as the support force. It normally consists of tanks and TOWs. Its job is to suppress all enemy units that can fire on the breach site and secure the near side of the obstacle. Artillery, mortars, and aviation support also can assist in this task. They either suppress

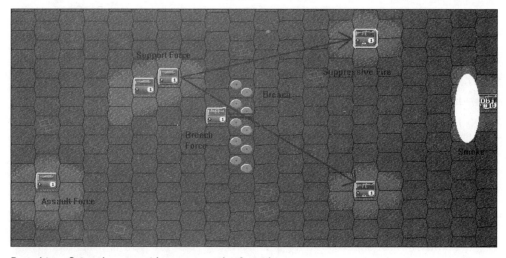

Breaching: Seize the near side, suppress the far side.

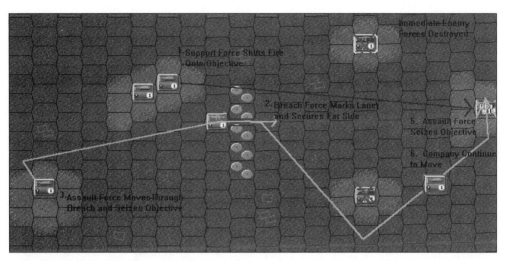

Seize the far side, and continue the mission.

or obscure the visibility of the enemy force to fire on the friendly force by firing HE or DPICM on identified enemy positions. They also place smoke on the enemy or block his line of sight toward the breach. As a third alternative, smoke the breach site itself with artillery, smoke generators, or onboard smoke. Feel free to use any or all of these methods as different games support them.

Second, designate the breaching force. The breaching force is usually infantry or engineers. They create and mark lanes through the enemy obstacles. After the lane is through, they provide local security on the far side of the obstacle.

Finally, the Assault Force moves through the gap and destroys the enemy on the objective.

The Support force may move through and widen the obstacle or assist the assault force. After the assault force moves through, the breaching force may also assist them. Once the breaching unit has seized its objective, additional follow on forces move through and continue the mission. Once through the breach you should prepare for a counter-attack by the enemy's local reserve.

Game Limitations

Most games do not allow the player to use all of these techniques. Neither *Tanks* nor *Armored Fist* allows you the flexibility with artillery that it really has. In *Tanks* the game automatically decides where to place artillery fire. In *Armored Fist* the player has to call for artillery from the tank view, and it only fires if there is a target. *Tigers on the Prowl*, on the other hand, does allow the player to place fires where and when he wants them. *M1 Tank Platoon* and *Tanks* allow the player to place smoke or artillery where desired, but do not play mines.

SUPPORTING ARMS

You use supporting arms—artillery, air defense, and air—to suppress the enemy, destroy or disrupt their units so you may attack them, or to screen forward movement of your forces.

In order to use artillery to destroy or disrupt the enemy, you must first have detailed knowledge of where the enemy is. This means you must move slowly and deliberately until you have spotted them. In *M1 Tank Platoon*, you can either do this by bounding forward or by using scout or attack helicopters. To screen your movement, you can either place smoke on known enemy positions or in between you and the enemy position.

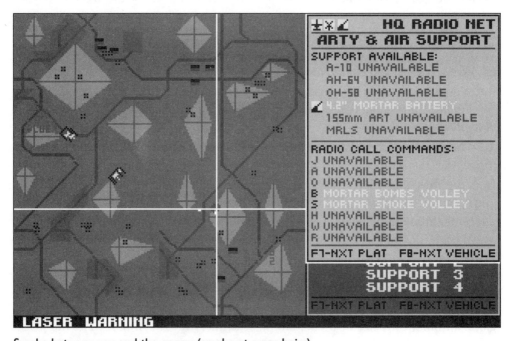

Smoke between you and the enemy (smoke at cross hairs).

In *M1 Tank Platoon* you have three types of artillery support: Mortars, 155mm Howitzers, and Multiple Launch Rocket Systems. Mortars are relatively small and most effective for attacking infantry and firing smoke missions. The 155 Howitzers also have two types of round, White Phosphorus and HE. WP builds a smoke screen quickly, but it dissipates rapidly. HE is good against light armored vehicles such as BMPs, but less so against main battle tanks. Finally, MLRS fires Improved Conventional Munitions that will explode as regular HE rounds if they hit a soft surface or as High Explosive Anti-Tank rounds if they hit a hard surface. They are effective against all types of targets.

If you have mortars and howitzers, first fire 155WP to build the smoke screen rapidly, then sustain it with the mortars. This builds a long duration smoke screen.

OL' SMOKY

Speaking of smoke, let's cover how to use the smoke grenades and engine smoke on the M1 and other vehicles. Use onboard smoke as a short term screening device to get you out of a fatal situation. A good example of this situation is the following: you are on a hilltop and begin receiving direct fire from enemy tanks or helicopters. Pop your smoke grenades and *back up*. Backing up places the smoke between you and the enemy. If you drive forward your own smoke highlights your vehicles and functions as a *shoot me* sign. This figure shows a smoke salvo from an M1 from the back. Notice the vehicle is screened from the front.

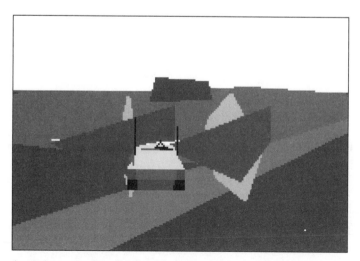

A smoke grenade salvo from behind a tank, so that from the front, the tank is obscured to the enemy.

Use engine smoke the same way. Sometimes you may want to use your M1's smoke to shield vehicles behind your lead platoon. For instance, you are attempting to get up on the objective and you want to shield your Bradleys or M113s from enemy fire. Place the M1s in line or wedge and the infantry in wedge behind them. Turn on the smoke and it will conceal them from enemy fire (of course, you may also lose one or two of your tanks). It is better to use artillery and place smoke in front of the enemy position instead of using your own smoke. The figures here show the screening effect of engine smoke. In the first, two Bradleys are behind the tanks. In the second you can see them just to the left of the last tank and to the right of the last smoke cloud.

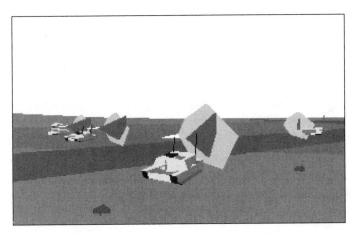

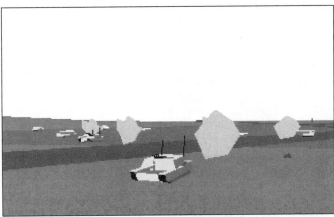

M1 Platoon screening M2's with engine smoke.

SMOKING GUN

Now, how do you use artillery to destroy the enemy? Again, you must first find the enemy. In the *M1 Tank Platoon* example, you can zoom down to maximum magnification and place the cross hairs on one vehicle to have the best chance of knocking someone out. Adjust the aim point after each volley. If you have two kinds of artillery support, shoot HE or MRLS at the target and use Smoke or WP to screen your advance (remember that you can see through smoke and the enemy can't). Continue the bombardment until your tanks are on top of the enemy. Then shift the fire to the most likely or known enemy positions. The final rounds of an actual prep are frequently marked with WP, or you can time it so the final rounds burst on the target as you drive up on the objective.

When firing artillery at a moving enemy, remember to time it so it will land on the enemy where he will be when the rounds come in instead of where he was when you called for it. Notice the smoke screen still in front of the enemy. However, in this next figure, you can see the tank coming up on the enemy while the artillery prep is still coming down.

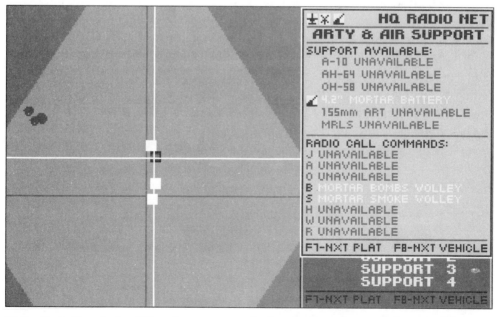

Notice that after placing HE on the enemy, smoke lingers along the enemy line of sight to your unit.

Coming in on the enemy right underneath the artillery prep.

HELICOPTERS AND CLOSE AIR SUPPORT

These weapons are essentially flying artillery. They can place a large amount of fire on the enemy. In *M1 Tank Platoon* they tend to overfly the target and get destroyed, so be careful. First find the enemy with your ground force, *then* call them in. If you have a scout helicopter, fly it forward to find the enemy, then send the attack helicopter or A-10 in toward the enemy. You can also use the results of its reconnaissance to find unguarded routes into the enemy rear. Scouts have a limited endurance, so call them only when you are sure of a target. They take a long time to return. Notice how the helicopter also uses hull down positions by flying very low and using the hill for cover. The figure here shows a hull down Apache scoring a hit.

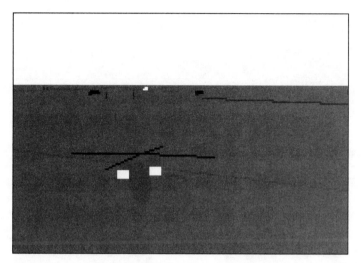

An Apache in hull down providing long distance support.

2

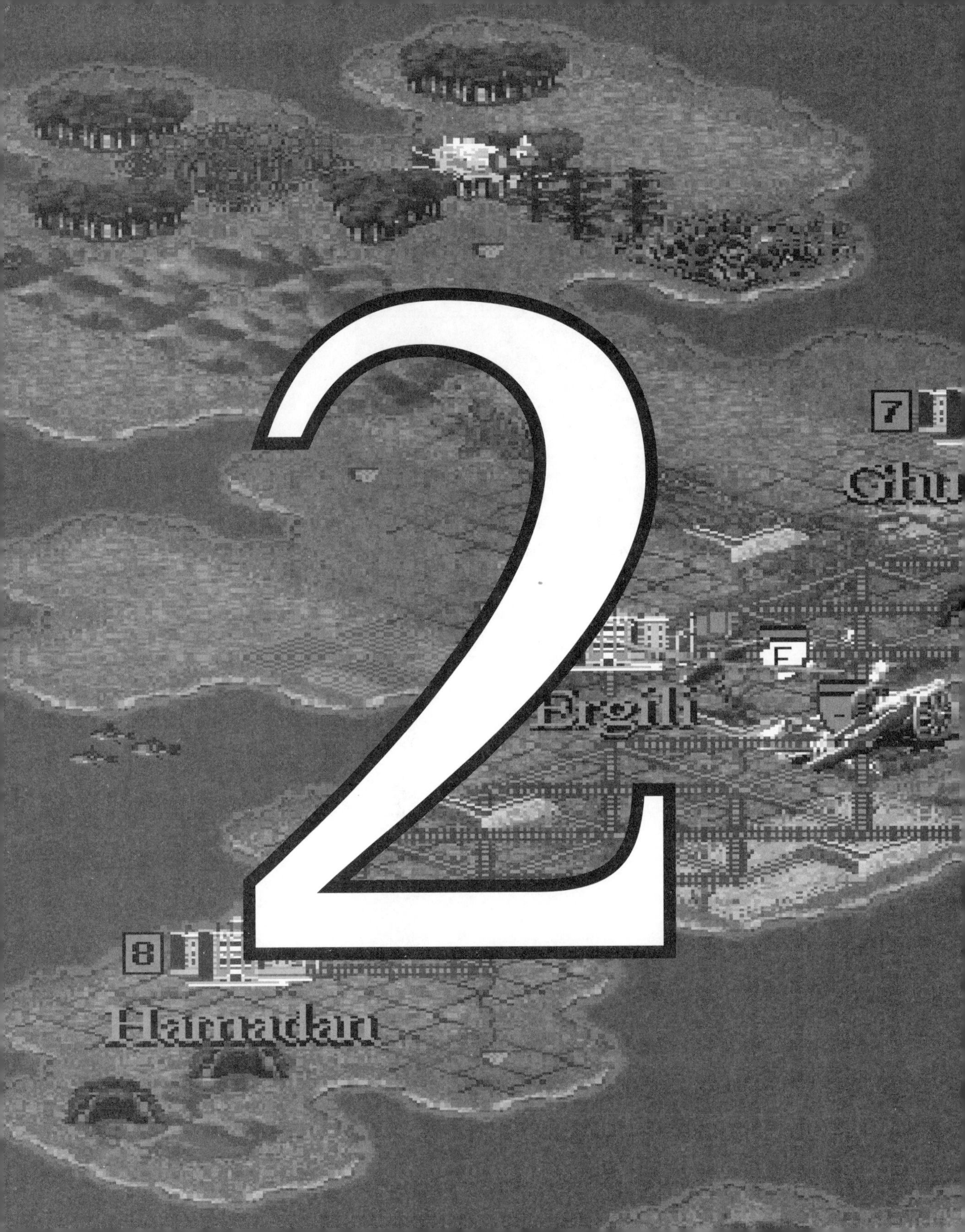

Civilization

II

Civilization II gives you the tools to rebuild civilization according to your vision of the world! You begin by building the world's first cities from the ground up and move into the space age by strategically organizing social, political, and military foundations that place you as the ruler of all you create.

TEN COMMANDMENTS FOR *CIVILIZATION II*

I went to the mountain, hoping for enlightenment. After climbing the steep slopes, the slippery goat paths, and avoiding the DOT crews painting lines on the trail, I arrived at the hermit's hut. Goody, I thought, he's in; the hand-lettered placard clearly read, "The Hermit is In." I looked closer and groaned; it actually said "The Hermit is Indisposed!" Oh well, I knocked on the old cardboard door anyway.

"What do you want? Go away!" I ignored the hermit's cries and pushed my way in anyway.

"Oh, great wise man, I must know the secret of *Civilization II*!" My lament was truly pitiful to hear, especially as I had laryngitis from shouting matches with hostile Greek diplomats. I waited anxiously for the old man's reply.

"Buy the hint book; it's a good 'un!"

"But I am poor, great prophet!"

"Hmm, well, I can give you a good deal on these tablets here. Fellow from the desert dropped in and said he didn't need 'em anymore; seemed no one was following 'em anyway." He rummaged about in a pile of tablets, scrolls, books, and

Nintendo cartridges. "Oh, drat, must have lost 'em. Here, try these. Didn't come from a bush or even a shrub, but they might do."

Eagerly, I reached down and took the heavy clay tablets. My awe and wonder were only slightly dimmed by the "©1996, Oracles–R–Us, Inc." embossed on the back. As I began to read, my eagerness turned to joy. Here, at last, was the wisdom I had sought. Besides, the tablets were just the right size to prop up that old coffee table I picked up last year at the yard sale. In cheap Hollywood Hestonese, here's what they said:

1. THOU SHALT OFFER PRAYERS TO FORTUNA, FOR SHE CAN CONTROL YOUR DESTINY.

Luck plays a vital role in *Civ II*, especially if you use the random features of the game's setup options. Even when you know how many civilizations you will face, and even who they are, luck is a powerful force. Most important are your starting conditions.

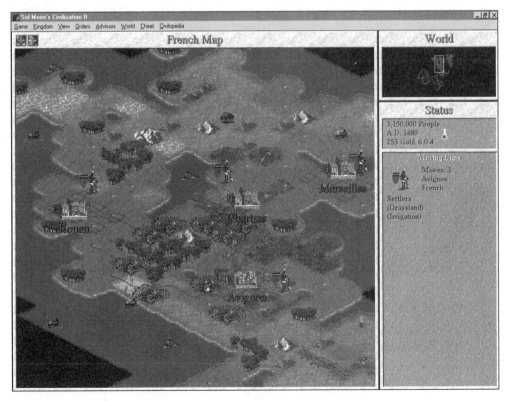

The humble Settler; you can never have too many.

Beginning your reign with one set tler in the midst of the tundra bodes ill for your future. Two settlers in fertile river valleys might not be nirvana—usually this means someone else is close by—but is a far better situation to be in. Likewise, those ubiquitous goody huts can make or break you. Always explore them, even deep in enemy territory. An extra city here, a mercenary unit there, a few gold pieces—all of this adds up, and it's free.

And of course, you can always hope that your rivals end up embroiled in neverending wars . . . and wars are the essence of luck; can you say "crap shoot?" Sure, I thought you could. Remember, it's better to be lucky than it is to be good, but being big, good, and lucky can't hurt.

Use terrain to your advantage.

2. THOU SHALT ALWAYS REMEMBER THAT EARLY GAINS PAY BIG DIVIDENDS LATER.

Think of it as an imperial savings account. An investment of cities and technology early allows you to build on a strong base and gain a leg up on your merciless foes as your efforts earn interest in the form of early civilization advances and better persuasive tools, like elephants and ironclads. With a good start you can endure slow-downs later, but it is almost impossible to play catch up from a weak beginning. Nothing cuts short a celebration in honor of the discovery of navigation so well as a sudden, unfriendly encounter with cruisers and battleships. The importance of laying a good foundation for growth cannot be overstated. You need to establish cities on the good sites on your starting continent as soon as possible, and develop them rapidly. Watch the historians; if your civilization is getting ratings of *puny* and *pin head*, you need to speed things up a bit.

Sometimes good fences make good neighbors.

3. THOU SHALT NOT DEVELOP HAPHAZARDLY.

Plan every city site, every advance, every build. It's all too easy to just click your way through centuries in a sort of daze, but that's a good way to lose big. Place cities where you can exploit special squares. Don't build improvements you don't need; churn out caravans for future use, or diplomats that have myriad uses in peace and war and don't require support. Research what you need, and plan your needs as much as possible. Keep a close eye on your opponents, and trade for needed technologies. Your foes will get there soon enough anyhow, so it's usually better to deal than to be stingy, and you might gain an ally while you are at it. Things not to give away: masonry, gunpowder, inventions (unless you already have Leonardo's garage up and going), and mobile warfare.

4. THOU SHALT NOT MAKE WAR UNLESS THOU ART SURE OF VICTORY.

Sure, you will be forced into war at times, but unless you can carry through to victory, play defensively and peacefully. War in *Civ II* is not pretty. With the new combat system, conflicts can drag on forever, but with the new technologies, fighting against a technologically superior foe is usually suicide. The proper way to wage war is to be dastardly and brutal. Amass superior force and position it for the attack well before precipitating a *causus belli*. Ideally, your troops will be poised to strike at several enemy cities at once, so you can grab a handful of vital cities and shock your foe into a peace treaty.

At low tech levels it is very hard to wage a protracted war and obtain decisive results; your troops just don't have the combat power to defeat walled cities. At high tech levels the same can be true, but proper use of howitzers, bombers, and of course the almighty nuke can show your enemies the true light of reason. Paratroopers are dramatic, but don't forget marines; an escorted transport or two loaded with leathernecks can seriously ruin a coastal empire's day. If you can gather the force and position it properly, don't worry about niceties like peace treaties—pull a Pearl Harbor and take the diplomatic lumps. War is not a casual affair in *Civ II*, so heed Machiavelli, who said that when one strikes at a prince, one must kill him. Fight to conquer, not to harass.

5. THOU SHALT ALWAYS USE THE BEST GOVERNMENT FOR THE SITUATION.

Unless you are well equipped with exotic wonders, waging war as a Democracy isn't a great idea. Similarly, trying to win the space race as a Monarchy is a royal farce. The

Modern living brings its own problems: pollution and neighbors more mighty than thou.

Statue of Liberty, with its ability to avoid anarchy during revolutions, is a great thing to have. As some players have noted, Fundamentalism is actually quite a good government for many circumstances. Though it takes a 50 percent hit on research, the incredible influx of money and the lack of unhappiness makes up for the lack of egghead activity rather nicely, making Fundamentalism the government of choice for warfare (unless you're playing version 1.07 or later). Communism isn't really good for much, and Republics are merely stepping stones to Democracy, though they can function as limited war systems in a pinch. Monarchy is a good general purpose government early in the game, but has too many limits to sustain growth. Don't be afraid to be revolting if necessary. One word of advice: if you've got lots of troops scouring the globe for the remnants of your inferior neighbors, don't switch to Democracy. Stick with a more violent civic structure until your troops come home.

6. THOU SHALT PREPARE FOR FUTURE WONDERS WELL IN ADVANCE.

Some wonders are just too good to allow anyone else to enjoy. Leonardo's Workshop, J.S. Bach's Cathedral, the Hoover Dam, Michelangelo's Cathedral—these things are intended only for those of the true faith. So, how to make sure the infidels don't get their grubby paws on your wonders? You can't prevent some poaching, but you can make it harder for them.

When on the verge of an advance that will let you build a particular wonder, start stockpiling those caravans and freight units. As soon as you can, rush those camels to the build site and raise the rafters pronto. If your foes beat you to the punch, and you've got other wonders available, switch over and build those rather than take the 50 percent hit on switching production. It is often better to keep a city building a wonder that is already built rather than trashing the shields, as long as you can roll the

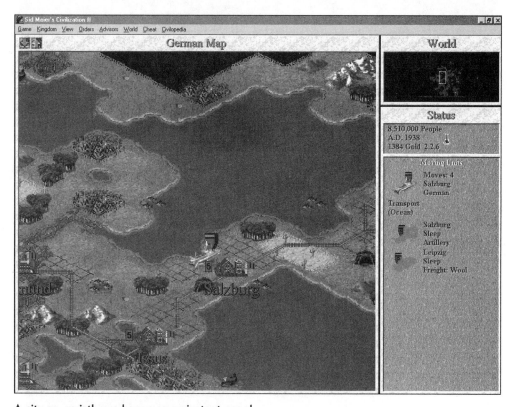

A city on an isthmus becomes an instant canal.

Sid Meier's Civilization II

Game Kingdom View Orders Advisors World Cheat Civilopedia

German Map   World

WONDERS OF THE INDUSTRIAL AGE

Leonardo's Workshop in Konigsberg (German)

J. S. Bach's Cathedral in Heidelburg (German)

Isaac Newton's College in Leipzig (German)

Adam Smith's Trading Co. in Nurnberg (German)

Darwin's Voyage (German)

The Eiffel Tower in Killdeer (Sioux)

WONDERS OF THE MODERN WORLD

Close

Status

000 People
1938
Gold 2.2.6

Moving Units

Moves: 3
Salzburg
German

Salzburg
No Orders
Artillery
Leipzig
No Orders
Freight: Wool
Salzburg
Fortified
Riflemen
Salzburg
Fortified
Riflemen

Kaiser Billy finally gets his place in the sun; all those Wonders give the ol' Civ score a boost.

production over into another wonder fairly soon. Just make sure you have some new wonders coming up sometime soon.

7. THOU SHALT DEFEND THY CITIES OR BE CAST INTO THE LAKE OF DIOXIN.

Many a codex and tome recommends two defensive units, but lo! Such is not enough. Two units plus an offensive unit, preferably a mobile one such as knights or elephants early; dragoons, cavalry, or armor later is the minimum garrison in times of trouble (which means about 90 percent of your reign). And, as my brother the shop foreman of the City Wall Builders Union, Local 213 says, "A city without a city wall ain't worth diddly squat."

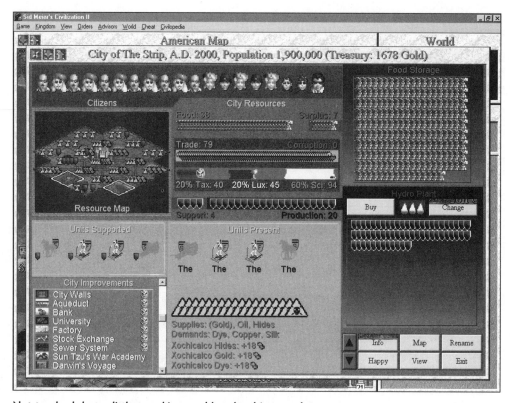

Not too bad, but a little tweaking could make this town hop.

While your foes waste their substance in futile assaults, your assault troops can sortie out and eliminate those pesky catapults and cannons with relative impunity. Besides, you never know when a stupid barbarian with horns on his head might be waiting around to be ransomed, and you don't want to be chasing him with a slug-like phalanx, do you? When Mr. Fission & Ms. Fusion come to play, however, either keep your unit density down or build SDI like crazy. Nothing ruins your day like watching the entire Babylonian Armored Corps go up in radioactive smoke.

8. THOU SHALT NOT LET THY WRATH MAKE THEE WROTH.

Or, just because some piss-ant civilization next door gets mad and makes war on you, you shouldn't lose sight of the big picture. As long as your cities are well defended (see Commandment 7) and your foe is truly ant-like, let their legions beat their swords

Nice and tidy, packed in like sardines but using space efficiently.

into plowshares (what the hell are plowshares asked this suburban boy?) upon your city walls. Eventually your neighbor will get tired and beg forgiveness. Be warned, though; once an enemy makes war on you, especially by sneak attack, they will probably continue to harass you. You might want to annihilate them on your lunch break.

9. THOU SHALT SPARE NO EFFORT TO IMPROVE THY MISERABLE EMPIRE QUICKLY.

In particular, make a beeline for Monarchy and then Invention. You need a king (no, not your Attitude advisor, the royal kind). You also need Leonardo's Workshop, unless you like rebuilding your military every few centuries. You need to expand the blight of your civilization to cover the continents with bawling babes and sprawling tenements, the better to overwhelm your enemies with armies, technology, and raw sewage. Build settlers early and often, as long as good city sites are near and you can defend what you build. Caravans are a necessity to win Wonder races, so Trade should be a high priority. Diplomats, and hence Writing, are great tools too, for peace and war, while a course that leads to Tactics can lead your troops to alpine heights of valor. Use your bagmen, er, diplomats, to corrupt, er, persuade foreign troops and barbarians to join your side; settlers make particularly good buys.

10. THOU SHALT ALWAYS CHEAT LIKE A RIVERBOAT GAMBLER.

After all, *you* are the Grand Wazoo here, and it's your fifty bucks. Want to try a hard line in diplomacy? Save first. Want to start a war? Save first. Don't be afraid to restart, either. Just consider it a bad dream brought on by undigested grain. Fiddle with the custom until you get a world you like. Steal ideas from folks on-line, and pretend they're your own. Keep restarting until you get the perfect setup, if you've got the patience. Play on weenie levels and cackle demonically as you dominate the world. Restart the game if you don't get a good starting location, preferably with lots of rivers. *Never* accept a game that makes you start in the Gobi desert, or in the frozen tundra. Use your spies to investigate foreign cities, then change their names to things like "Loserville" and "Privytown" (yes, you can really do this!). Above all, have fun.

AND THERE WAS MORE . . .

Scribbled on the back in black felt tip were lottery numbers, horoscopes, and a hot tip for the third race at the Aqueduct, but I could make out a few useful items. One, scrawled in terrible Babylonian, noted that later versions of *Civ II* included nifty things like a visible city radius in the grid view and autopilot settlers. Another, block printed in Aramaic, reminded would-be world beaters that sometimes just surviving until the end of the game was accomplishment enough, especially when playing against kings or better. A Phoenician passage warned against building impenetrable walls of fortresses on your frontiers, lest you keep out not only your neighbors but your neighbors' caravans as well.

The most interesting item in this collection of addenda, however, was a brief paragraph in passable Assyrian, which included the following tips:

★ Build cities on rivers, as you get great trade production and your sewage flows away from the palace.

* Don't pick fights with all your neighbors at once, or you will die.

* It's easy to provoke your neighbors into starting a war by refusing all of their requests and demanding tribute all the time.

* Never, never, never draw into an inside straight.

Finally, I thought to myself, the wisdom of the ages is truly in my hands. Now, I would no longer have to endure the humiliation of paying tribute to Gandhi, of fleeing from the armies of France, of having to let the Americans beat me to the punch on all the best Wonders. Visions of world conquest danced in my head. Maybe with this knowledge I could advance even, dare I hope, to playing at Prince level? Nothing seemed too outrageous now.

"Thank you oh great hermit," I said as I bowed while trying to avoid bending too close to the old man, who obviously had never heard of modern personal hygiene products. "How can I ever repay you?"

The old fellow got a faraway look in his eye as he said to me. "Well, you can start by getting off my foot. You've been standing on it for half an hour." With that he pushed me out of his tent. As I tumbled the forty leagues down the mountain trail, clutching my prize, I passed another pilgrim making his way to the old hermit's hut. "Hey," he shouted as I rolled past, "did you find out the secret of life?" All I could do as I hurtled down the slope was call out "Yeah! Don't build cities in the desert, and remember that a pair of stealth bombers always beats three triremes!"

CIVILIZATION II DESIGN TIPS

"Blast! That's the third destroyer I've lost to an ironclad today. Well, we'll soon fix that!" Taking his trusty notepad in hand, Sam set to work editing his RULES.TXT file as the computer went ta-pocketta-pocketta-pocketta-pocketta . . . *Civilization II* stands apart from most games of its genre by putting the graphics, data and even rules for much of the game out in an easily accessible format that we can change to our Turkish Delight (I hope the *Master of Orion II* programmers are paying attention).

As a consequence, there are a number of player-created scenarios already out there, but if you're like most strat-gamers, you like to tinker, have strong opinions on what feels right, and you won't be satisfied until you have massaged the numbers yourself and given that last little tweak to the graphics.

DON'T TOUCH THAT DIAL!

Right now, before you touch anything, make backup copies of the UNITS.GIF and RULES.TXT files to another directory. Yes, you can re-install the game, but that's a pain and then you have to redo the latest patch and all that jazz. Life's too short, back it up.

Twiddling the rules file can be done with any ASCII editor, *Notepad* is as good as any. Make sure you save your work as a straight text file with the .TXT extension. Rolling your own graphics is a horse of a different feather. While the units file has a normal .GIF extension, it is a specific type of .GIF and only certain graphics programs can correctly save that type of file (87a, to be precise). *Paint Shop Pro* (PSP), version 3.12 (*not* 3.11, it won't work) can save the file correctly and is very easy to work with. It is widely available for download on most online services as shareware.

Reducing digitized images to use as units is a problematic process. By the time the graphic has been brought down to the correct size it is a mush of pixels only vaguely

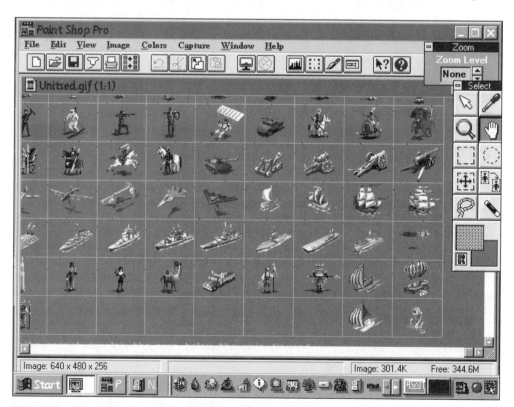

Paint Shop Pro makes it easy to work with and save the GIF file.

reminiscent of the original photo. You can still use the result as a template and redo it using colors from the image palette from the units .GIF. No new colors may be added.

The general procedure is: find the icon of a the unit you want to replace (you can only overlay an icon for one of the existing units or one of the three user-defined slots). Tweak and edit the icon you're creating while taking care not to mess up the green lines or going beyond the boundaries of the light purple rhombus your icon rests upon. Save your work and you're done. Since you have to use a slot that already has a unit icon in it, you can use the existing graphic as a guide. In a similar vein, new sounds must bear the name of the old unit's sound that you're replacing.

MODIFYING RULES

The top section of the rules file contains global variables, which will have massive effects on the way *Civilization II* plays. For example, lowering the amount of food each

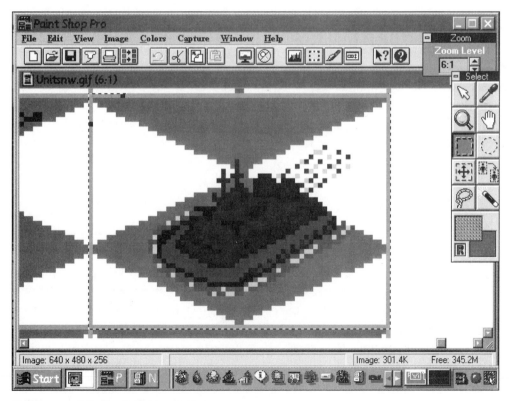

Modify an existing unit slot to create your own.

person eats per turn to one will allow massive cities to exist, and lessen the urgency of dealing with unhappy citizens. For example, you can reduce the amount of food eaten by settlers to one in all cases, raise the threshold for sewer systems to fourteen (twelve seems too close to eight), and increase the number of free units for Communism to seven. You can also change the tech paradigm to 15. As it plays, we are usually well ahead of the historical track for discoveries and this change lets us *savor* the fruits of our research longer before the next development erases the thrill from memory.

Some people also reduce the penalty in science for Fundamentalist governments by entering a lower number in the "max effective science rate" area. Try putting in zero, especially if you like being a ruthless dictator (Democracies are just too whiny).

The next section lists all the techs and their interrelationships. While you can tinker with all the details here, be careful in the way you tweak anything having to do with how the AI will see things. You can radically affect the game and thus create silly results. There are also three tech slots open for your use. Entries here will not display properly in the game, but they *will* activate properly, so you'll just have to remember that your new tech of Clown Makeup requires Feudalism and Diplomacy, is required for Combined Arms and gives you the nuclear pie launcher unit.

Next we have cost, upkeep, and requirements for all the city improvements and wonders. While there is no facility for creating your own wonders and improvements separately, you have the consolation of being able to adjust the cost, maintenance, etc. for those that exist. When changing the cost, remember that this number is multiplied by ten.

By the way, when making any changes which require you to enter the abbreviation for an advance, enter it exactly as it is shown in the tables including capitalization; otherwise, the program won't recognize the abbreviation.

Now we come to some of the good stuff. The entries here list which advancement causes a wonder to expire, if any. If it says "nil," then that wonder never expires. Here you might try removing the expiration dates from Leonardo's Workshop, the Hanging Gardens, the Colossus, and King Richard's Crusade. Changing the latter three allows you to actually want to build them instead of going "That's nice" when their advance is discovered.

At last come the units themselves. Here you can make lots of changes. Consider increasing the movement for settlers and engineers by one each, and give engineers the explorer road bonus. Raise mech infantry's attack to seven, since it seems silly that cavalry, dragoons, and other antiquated units are better in combat than mech infantry.

Now they can attack with a good chance of success, or at least of wounding their target severely.

Raise Destroyers' attack and defense by one, giving them a satisfactory edge over ironclads, but leaving them still easily trounced by cruisers. You can make other changes, such as removing cruisers' ability to spot subs, but subs can gain that advantage, as well as carriers, to reflect the other assets a carrier has that aren't reflected in the game.

Change Bombers so they are now introduced with the Flight advance along with fighters. Advanced Flight can be changed to grant two new units: the jet bomber and jet fighter, which are made obsolete by Stealth technology. Hovercraft have also been added, letting you (and the computer) make surprise raids. Hovercraft can move eleven spaces if you have Nuclear Power and Magellan's Voyage. There are also stats for a Zeppelin unit that you can replace the explorer with. It is possible to make a nuclear attack sub, but then you'd have to replace another unit.

CREATING NEW UNITS

Creating a new unit or reworking an old one is simple. The only difficulty is keeping the numbers and entries straight so you don't create settlers with an endurance of two turns and a bombing attack of twelve. Just replace the entries for one unit (or the user defined slots) with the data of your choosing and voila!—instant new unit. By the way, air units don't need the "ignore city walls" bonus, because air units already do so by their nature, though it doesn't hurt them to have that flag turned on.

Consider doing something about aircraft; in particular, bombers. Given the time scale of the game, it seems ridiculous to have bombers sitting out there as clay pigeons for a year and then only letting them have one attack, when fighters have as many as they want and get to fly back home for a brew. The only way to rectify this is to give bombers all their movement in one turn, but then they appear to fly *faster* than fighters. If you want to correct things anyway, here's how to make the change: find the bomber units stats in the rules file. Now look for an eight followed by a period, then a comma, then a two and another comma. Change the eight to sixteen and the two to a one and save the file. Now your bombers will be holy terrors from the sky . . . but so will the computer's. Use the same procedure to change the stealth bomber, if you like.

As for the terrain section and the leader stuff, you can take one of the tribes and change all the names and titles to suit yourself just by typing replacements. Remember to keep the columns aligned so the program can find things. Terrain can be transmogrified, but be judicious in the values you choose and, as always, make sure that everything is in its proper place.

3

Command & Conquer

W

ell, troops, you'd think that after two alien incursions we humans would have enough of warfare, but here we find ourselves facing an even greater threat from within in the form of the Brotherhood of Nod. Welcome to this, the first United Nations Global Defense Initiative (GDI) Veteran Lecture Series. For those of you who've transferred over from *X-COM* (even if temporarily, for Intelligence reports that a third alien incursion is likely), fighting with the GDI will require a change in the way you *do business*, and for those of you new to military operations, get ready for an experience unlike anything you've had before.

BASES

With the GDI, you'll face operations more intense, faster-paced, and more involved than those discussed in previous Lecture Series. As a GDI commander, you'll control more forces, more weapons platforms, and have more decisions than you would have as an X-COM commander. Now base construction, unit, and system construction and management have dropped down to the tactical level—no longer can you blithely go off on a mission knowing that your bases are safe while you're away; now you may have to juggle construction, management, and defense at the

same time you are issuing orders to individual troops. While it appears that Westwood (creators of your interface software nicknamed *Command & Conquer*, or *C&C* for short) has assembled pretty good intelligence on the technology you'll face (see the Field Manual included with the *C&C* software), it's still too early in the fight to know just how all that technology will interact on the battlefield. This chapter will cover some of the basics of base creation and defense at the violent tactical level.

BASE ISSUES

On many missions you'll be required to establish, maintain, and/or capture base facilities from which to mount your operations. Because bases are thrust into the tactical level of combat, you will need to pay very close attention to base defense and all the related issues: terrain layout, proximity to enemy forces, relation to supplies of Tiberium, possible exploitation of existing structures, base growth, etc.

Some missions won't involve basing issues for your forces. Missions we've encountered so far include those where you must establish a base from the ground up, those where you take over an existing GDI base (or perhaps have to reinforce one), and those that give you the opportunity to capture Nod facilities (any mission that involves both GDI and Nod facilities in the same area of operations raises the possibility of facility capture).

ESTABLISH A NEW BASE

If your mission requires you to establish a new base, part of your initial force mixture will be a mobile construction vehicle (MCV). Your primary goal at this point is to DEFEND THE MCV. This cannot be stressed enough—if you lose your MCV you'll not be able to start your base, and unless you have Engineers with which to capture enemy facilities, you might as well abort your mission. At this point in the mission you should adopt tactics from naval operations—consider your MCV the *aircraft carrier*, with all your other forces in a ring around it (or at least between it and any avenues of approach Nod forces might use). Keep the MCV away from any fighting, and do not use it to help scout for suitable base sights—use your other forces for this (especially fast light vehicles if you have them).

Your first job is to scout for a site for the base (while defending against initial Nod assaults against your beach head). Carefully consider the terrain. Are there ridgelines or cliff faces that enemy ground troops can't cross? Defensive terrain like this is wonderful because, unlike even the strongest fortification walls, it cannot be breached. If

Here's an example of good base positioning.

you can get these natural barriers on one or two sides of your base, your defense job will be much easier. Note, however, that such terrain also limits the mobility of your own forces and your base expansion possibilities (you can't move or expand across it), so plan carefully. Ideally, your site will have plenty of room for expansion—lots of clear terrain with no trees.

Many missions will require you to raise extra funds to support your operations; this means you'll need access to a supply of Tiberium. While you can collect Tiberium some distance from your base and haul it back for processing, this is less than ideal. Your harvesters are more vulnerable to enemy attack when they have to travel long distances (requiring you to dedicate defensive forces to them for longer periods of time), and you will have to wait longer for fresh supplies of Tiberium. It is better to place a base near an area rich in Tiberium; although, it shouldn't necessarily be directly adjacent to a Tiberium field. Tiberium seems to be somewhat unstable in its raw form and may explode when exposed to gunfire, causing collateral damage in nearby facilities and to troops!

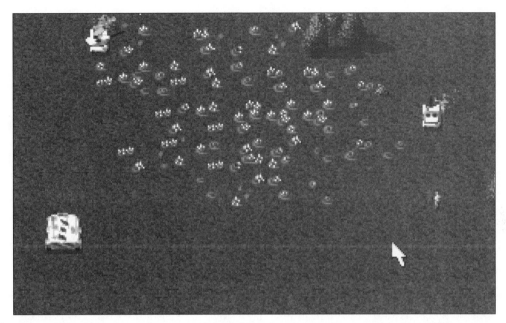

Watch out! This Tiberium field isn't a good place for a base; it's not very large and won't last too long.

While you may be eager to plant your MCV and start your base as soon as you find a Tiberium field, you should consider several items first: the first Tiberium field you find may not be very extensive, and you could exhaust it quickly, leaving you far from another source. Continue scouting; you may even find another field not too distant, and you can plant your base midway between them. The first field you find may not be in ideal terrain, or may be too near (or too far) from enemy forces and/or your objective. However, don't wait so long to find an *ideal* site that your force is weakened so much that it can't defend your base while it is still under construction.

Once you've planted your base, consider its immediate and long term growth. Particularly valuable facilities (construction yard, powerplant, refinery, etc.) should be placed near defensive terrain if available or away from the expected direction of enemy attacks. Refineries should be as close to the supply of Tiberium as is possible and safe, but should not project out too far from the core of the base (or should be heavily defended, by troops at first and defensive facilities later on. Plan for the placement of defensive sites (Guard Towers, fortifications etc.), leaving room for expanding rings of defenses as your base grows. Be careful of putting all your initial funds into base growth. Instead, only build enough initial facilities to enable you to refine

Tiberium and produce fresh troops. If you're able to hold off Nod forces and can start processing the Tiberium, then you can expand with more exotic facilities.

EXISTING FACILITIES

In some missions you'll be required to take over existing facilities. Here, of course, you'll have to rely on the judgement of the previous commander, and hope the facility is well designed. Often, however, the very fact that you're taking over means things won't be ideal; either the previous commander was incompetent and probably placed the base poorly, or is injured, dead, or captured, which means the base has been or still is under Nod attack (and may be in poor shape). You may even be leading a relief force to a base that has been out of contact with GDI headquarters; in such an operation we may not even know the exact location of that base anymore, and you'll have to scout just to find it.

Generally, when you take over an existing facility your first priority should be to secure the area (which may include jumping into the fray of an on-going Nod attack). Once the base is safe (for the moment), take stock of its situation: has Tiberium collection and processing stopped? What is the condition of the facilities? How are your

Taking over the enemy's digs.

defenses? If you've been allocated extra funds for this mission, put them into getting the refinery and barracks back into full working order (saving some if possible to help replenish your troop strength). If Tiberium collection and processing has stopped, find out why: do you just need to repair/rebuild the refinery, or has local supply of Tiberium been used up? If the latter is the case, you will need to go scout the area for another source. As you are restoring the facilities and the Tiberium processing, keep an eye out for new Nod attacks—you are vulnerable right now, and Nod will be certain to make use of the opportunity if possible.

CAPTURING NOD FACILITIES

Any mission that has a force mix that includes Engineers (or that lets you produce them) opens up the possibility of capturing Nod facilities and putting them to GDI use (or at least denying them to Nod). In fact, in some of your missions this may be your only goal—you may be given Engineers but no MCV, so if you want to capture a GDI base at the end of your operation, you'll have to assault with Engineers. Engineers are defenseless against Nod forces, so do not send them up against a Nod base unsupported. As a first step, you should use your Engineers to capture any construction yards or Fists of Nod (the Nod equivalent of our barracks).

The base is restored—now we can bring the fight to Nod!

Deciding what you will capture first depends on the tactical situation. If the Nod commander is focusing on cranking out forces, you'll want to capture the Fists first (otherwise you risk losing anything you capture to newly produced Nod forces). On the other hand, if the Nod commander has plenty of funds available and if you capture the Fists but leave the Construction Yard available, he or she may just build new Fists. It's your call; you may even want to combine facility capture and facility destruction. If you capture the Fists, destroy the Power Plants so Nod must first build new Power Plants before new Fists, or if you capture the Construction Yard(s), destroy the Fists (you can always build more). Whatever you do capture at least one Construction Yard for GDI use. Once you've captured all the Construction Yards and Fists of Nod, the rest of the Nod base is basically at your mercy—you can capture or destroy it as your mission requires (although be on the lookout for possible Nod reinforcements!).

Now let's focus our attention on the more critical aspect of our game plan: assaults on Nod bases.

BASE ASSAULTS

Nod bases are usually well laid out, in defensive terrain with few access points, and are heavily defended. Often even cutting off Nod access to Tiberium is not enough to dry a base up; the Brotherhood holds such an overwhelming amount of Tiberium world-wide that individual base commanders often have access to an excess of funding with which to purchase and fly in new weapons, materiel, and troops. A simple siege may not be enough; a direct assault is often your only option.

Of course, our missions tend to vary widely, both in objectives and resources, so there is no *right* way to hit a base each time. Before charging into a particular situation, take stock: is your primary mission to assault the base, or is it to protect something else? In your assault, do you need to take or destroy the whole base, or just a portion of it? Perhaps you need to perform a *snatch-and-grab* of something (or someone) in the base. What are your forces—are you using regular troops, Engineers, commandos, vehicles, and/or long-range weaponry? Are you operating from (and do you need to defend) a base of your own?

What about the enemy setup? Do you know where the Nod base is? What are the approaches? Defensive emplacements? Troops strengths? Where are the Tiberium fields Nod is harvesting, and can you interdict them? Can Nod air-drop troops behind your lines? *Is there more than one Nod base?* Worst of all, might this Nod base be one containing some of the weapons of mass destruction (WMD) our intelligence has gotten hints of?

SURVEY THE SITUATION

Before you can even begin to think about sending a major assault force towards a base you need to gather information on it. First, you must pinpoint its location in your area of operations (this is not a trivial task in rugged terrain). You'll need to scout out at least one (and ideally more) path from your base or beachhead to the Nod facility. Probe around the perimeter of the base; find out what avenues of approach exist, where its entrances are, and what and where are its perimeter defenses. In this phase try to avoid combat—you want to send your scouts in and out without attracting attention. If your scouts are discovered, *don't* extract them back in the direction of your base or beachhead. You don't want to draw Nod's attention down on you yet. Instead, have them pull away to another part of the area of operations (ideally an area you haven't

Engineers are placed safely behind the force, and Guard Towers protect against counter-attack from the rear.

explored yet—they can always look for other Nod facilities, Tiberium deposits, or even a *backdoor* approach to the Nod base).

For this phase you should only use two or three troops or light vehicles. While something like a Humm-vee may be much faster, it is also more likely to attract the Nod's attention. Most likely you'll be using Minigun or Grenade infantry troops; they're faster than the others and, frankly, more expendable. If you're *very* lucky, you'll have been assigned one of our rare commandos (although if you have a commando, he's probably also your assault force, so keep him away from vehicles and gun emplacements). Once your forces have scouted the perimeter (avoiding the interior for now, as that's a sure way to stir up the Nod forces) you can either send them to scout other portions of the area of operations or just pull them back a bit to keep an eye on Nod movements (especially if you don't have a comm center built) and an initial *speed bump* against premature Nod aggression.

THE BUILDUP

As you are scouting the Nod base, you should be preparing your assault force(s). If you don't have a base with which to train or build new forces, your build-up options are limited. You may get reinforcements, but you can't always rely on this. If you're without a base but are still expected to capture or destroy the Nod base, you'll be given Engineer troops—these units are critical, so protect them! Arrange your assault force so that such weak-but-important forces (missile launchers also fit into this category) are preceded into the assault by more mobile, defensible, and/or expendable units. If you do have a base, don't expend all your funds building an assault force before your scouting is done. Save funds for the end of the scouting phase in case the scouts discover a new threat at the last minute.

If you can, position your forces to assault from more than one direction at once. Look for areas that are near the base but that can't access it directly due to terrain obstructions or barriers; you can position medium or long-range forces (like Rocket infantry or missile launchers) here. If you have them, consider using transport helicopters to move forces in behind the Nod base, but beware of getting too close to a base with SAM sites!

THE ASSAULT

Consider your assault: should it be in waves or one massive push? If you're performing a *snatch 'n run* mission, you'll only need to penetrate the base once, but you'll

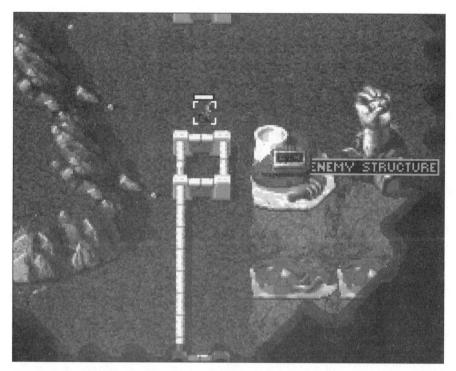

Commandos are rare, but they can scout wider territory swatches and destroy buildings.

need to make a fighting withdrawal—you may need to assign forces to cover your backside. These are the kind of missions where your most likely to get a commando assigned to your force (in fact, you may have *only* a commando). Commandos can take out individual troops at great distances, usually with one shot. They can easily blow up weapons emplacements and major buildings, but they are vulnerable to concerted attacks by enemy vehicles. If you have air power assigned to you, use it against the base (especially if the base has a Tower of Light or nukes); watch out for those SAM sites though.

The more advanced the Nod weapons emplacements, the more power they need—taking out several power generation plants may be enough to cripple his base. Often these power generation facilities are located towards the rear of a Nod base, behind weapons emplacements and protected from direct assault by barriers, terrain, and/or the edge of the operations area. If you can, punch a hole in the barriers (using Grenade/Rocket infantry and or tanks/missile launchers) so you can insert a secondary force to attack these vulnerable facilities.

Three critical types of facilities are the Fists of Nod, the Airstrips, and the Construction Yard. The order that you capture or destroy these depends on the situation at the time of the assault. If the Nod commander is producing waves of infantry, try taking out the Fists; if you're force is short on vehicles with which to take on new Nod vehicles, take out the Airstrip(s). His construction yard can be particularly important; take that out and he can't reconstruct his buildings and weapons emplacements. If you are to capture the base intact, make certain you first take out his ability to produce new troops or receive new vehicles (but be ready to quickly follow up with an assault on his construction yard!).

If capture doesn't matter, destroy or sell off the buildings as soon as you capture them (and don't waste your expensive Engineers on such cheap facilities as Power Plants (unless you need to take it out quickly) and silos. While it may be tempting to take out his Tiberium Refinery, it's not critical—often Nod has so much other revenue that a base commander likely won't miss the Tiberium (in the short-run). Instead, it is easier for you to assault his Harvesters when they are away from the base.

SPECIAL ARTIFICIAL INTELLIGENCE WEAKNESSES

As you know, because of a shortage of senior commanders and apparent advancements in artificial intelligence (AI) technology, both Nod and GDI have developed computer-commanded bases. Ironically, both sides seem to have the same set of weaknesses in the AI they've developed, so while you'll want to use the following information for your own benefit, you must do all you can to keep it from falling into enemy hands.

For some reason, the AI commanders are loathe to breach even sandbag obstacles. Because of this, if your mission has you commanding a GDI base with the capability to produce barriers, you can use this Nod weakness to keep his forces away from your base and even bottled up in areas of your choosing. Build a barrier (use sandbags because they're cheapest and easiest to build and they work) towards the Nod base. Remember, you always need to build a facility—even a sandbag barrier–next to another GDI facility; of course, once you've built two or three in a row you can start selling off the ones at the start of the line, effectively *leap-frogging* a wall towards the Nod base. You can block the AI from crossing rivers by leaving a sandbag in the middle of a ford, you can build a wall across a valley entrance to keep him from coming down an avenue of approach, or you can even build a wall across the entrance to his base!

Whatever you do, the AI commander won't intentionally undo it (secondary explosions during combat may accidentally breach a wall for him, so be on the lookout for

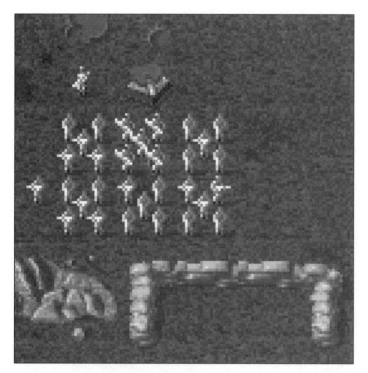

Battling the AI commander.

this). If you block off a point that your forces will need to use, don't worry—you can always just sell off some of the bags, let your forces through, and then plug the hole. One trick is to build a wall near his base, blocking in all his troops. Then, build a second line of fortifications just out of range of his defenses—sandbags first, and then Guard Towers and troops or vehicles. Sell off one of the sandbags in the line nearest his base; his pent-up troops will stream out, right into the crossfire of your Guard Towers (for infantry) and your troops and vehicles (for vehicles). Of course, if he has long-range WMD—like the Tower of Light—or nuclear missiles, this assault tactic won't work, but you can still block him in with sand bags.

Another weakness of the AI (and inexperienced human) commanders is an over-reaction to assaults on his Tiberium harvesters. If you hit his harvester with just a minigunner, he'll tend to send most of his mobile forces to its defense, leaving his base with only fixed defenses (and these, if they are in range of the units assaulting the harvester, may ignore everything else as well). You can even combine these two weaknesses: use sandbags to block in his harvester away from his base. Then, hit it with a weak unit (i.e., don't destroy his harvester; if you do the AI reassigns his forces), and wait while he sends his mobile forces far away from his base, leaving it open to your main assault force.

SHOW TIME!

Well, that's it folks. As always, time is precious, so return to your commands. Good luck, straight shooting, and a safe journey through to the end of our conflict.

Remember, your mission may not require you to actually destroy or occupy a whole base.

Afterlife

A h, *lost souls*. Most preachers would lead you to believe this means poor chumps who made bad decisions and ended up in the hot place. In *Afterlife*, ending up in hell isn't so bad, and making the grade to enter heaven isn't much better. In fact, a steady stream of stuff-of-unending-life (souls) going to hell (and heaven) helps to keep the pennies flowing. Lost souls are really dead men who haven't had their particular afterlife needs met, and who walk off into limbo. Too many of these can truly make the life of an aspiring Demiurge . . . hell.

THE ART OF KEEPING DEAD MEN FROM WALKING

On the road to heaven or hell—it's your choice—you'll meet everyone from the Disco Demon to Aria the Afterlife Advisor. But whichever route you choose, always keep your Heavenly Scent Atomizer in sight.

THE BASIC YIN-YANGS OF HEAVEN AND HELL

CD-ROM
Check out the CD-ROM
included in this book for the demo
version of *Afterlife*.

Remember that in this game, heaven means a nice, cushy afterlife and hell means a rough, painful existence forevermore (well, not always, depending on a soul's belief system). Short roads with diverse fates are for

Manually balancing fate structures will save pennies early in the game.

heaven; long, confusing walks to one's well-separated punishments are the rule in hell.

A good initial itinerary of structures in both heaven and hell will include a gate, a 3x3 block of fate tiles for all seven fates, a topia, a training center, a siphon, a karma station anchor with connecting karma track and karma portal anchor, two ports, and maybe a bank. Almost all of these structures will need to be connected to a road, except fate zoning, which should be within three tiles of a road. Remember to connect siphons to rocks.

Each structure puts out vibes, which affect the structures around it. As you'd expect in heaven, good vibes are pro-evolution and bad vibes hinder the evolution of neighboring structures. In hell the opposite is conveniently true. Make frequent use of the microview function to get building descriptions and mapview function to keep tabs on how your structures are affecting each other. Note that gates emit counter evolutionary vibes. Training centers or topias are good structures to place near gates, to help cancel out the negative effects.

Lost souls in the initial portion of the game are generally related to fate zoning deficits. If a spike appears, change the tempo immediately to divine intervention (a good habit to get into whenever there's trouble), and flatten the tiles. Make sure the fate tiles are within three tiles of a road, all roads are connected, enough siphons are available (use mapview again) to make sure the zoning is charged, and that there's no counter evolutionary karma portal anchor nearby.

A WELL-TRAINED PRINCIPAL IS HARD TO FIND

The quantity and quality of your labor force of angels and demons will affect the success of the game greatly. If fiery haloes start showing up in heaven, or golden haloes in hell, too many workers are idle; this will result in much destruction. Not enough workers means higher labor costs from a larger imported labor force. Training centers will regulate these situations to some degree. In the training center microview, the centers can be toggled to accept a certain percentage of applicants. Angel Quotient (AQ)

Higher acceptance rates mean more but less efficient workers at training centers.

and Demon Quotient (DQ) are a grade of the efficiency of the workers. A high acceptance rate will turn out more angels and demons, but with lower efficiency. Being more selective will result in more intelligent and efficient workers. Efficiency rates can vary between 50-150. A good starting point is a 50 percent acceptance rate and AQ's and DQ's of around 100.

Topias and Ports are also regulators of the work force. Topias house your work force and need to be monitored, so that new ones can be built or existing ones upgraded as they become filled. Ports hold large amounts of angels and demons. They're good to lay down when there's trouble involving workers who need to be reduced in a hurry.

Planetary Intervention

Not only does a budding Demiurge have to worry about heaven and hell, but there's also a whole planet undergoing disasters and slowly making its way to nuclear

Fates can be close together in heaven, but placing them close to gates and anchors is a mistake.

technology to worry over. It's tempting to alter technology because it increases population over time, but the higher the technology the greater the threat of nuclear war. High technology levels are best countered by increased peacefulness on the planet. Tampering with sin/virtue levels is best done in small measures and with frequent game saves. Be ready to counter an unexpected result of a sin/virtue change with its corresponding opposite.

Disasters will impact heaven and hell frequently. Floods, earthquakes, and similar events will lead to the rapid influx of souls into the afterlife. Once again, reducing the tempo to insure there are enough gates, fate zones, and workers to handle the increased population will make the best of the situation.

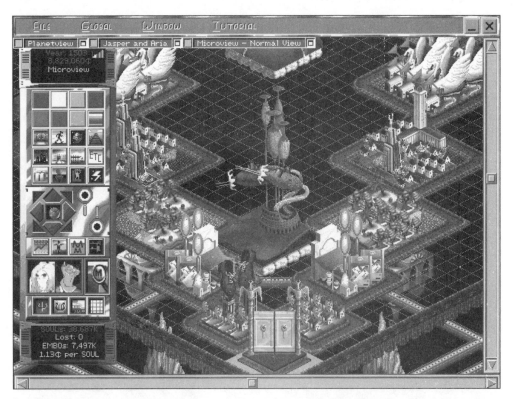

Special buildings like the Heavenly Scent Atomizer keep away Bad Things and should be placed in strategic locations.

THE NICE THING ABOUT
SPECIAL BUILDINGS AND BAD THINGS

Special buildings repel bad things. Heaven's Vista Enhancement Doohickey will shoot down Birds of Paradise for a radius of eight tiles, while hell's Ugliness Engine will waste Bats Out of Hell at the same range. Heaven's Audio Improving Embophone will protect against the Blues at a range of about nine tiles, and hell's Crinkly Cacophony Contrivance will repel a Disco Demon at a similar radius. Heaven's Paradise Pair O' Dice will be repelled by the Fluffy Comfort Dispenser for about a 12-tile radius, and hell's Tactile Degradation Gizmo will keep the Freeze at bay at the same range. Heaven's Scent Atomizer and hell's Flatulence Ol-Factory will keep the Nose at bay at around 10 tiles out. The Basket is countered for approximately 11 tiles by the Creamy Candy Castle in heaven, and by the Wellspring of Unsavoriness in hell.

When a billion souls are reached in heaven and hell, Omnibolges and Love Domes are granted. These structures are very tempting to lay down because they're essentially perfectly balanced, self-regulating mini-heavens and hells that offer nice, pro-evolutionary vibes for a whopping 16 tile radius. No fuss, no muss, even the labor cost is paid for by The Powers That Be. Note though that these structures can take a big bite out of the population of other fate tiles; this may lead to all the usual woes of unemployed workers. In addition, their occupants are not included for Soul Rate computations. Fortunately, admission rates can be adjusted just like training centers. Planning ahead by reducing the number of available workers and re-evaluating current zoning can minimize these structures' negative effects.

Listen to Jasper and Aria, they generally have good advice.

There is one nice thing about Bad Things: they can be toggled off! Don't be a macho Demiurge who has to play tough all the time. Sure, you take a hit on the Soul Rate, but toggling off the Bad Things for a time, especially in the middle portion of the game when money is tight, may help you reach that 1 billion served mark.

DON'T FORGET JASPER AND ARIA

Afterlife provides advisors in the form of Jasper and Aria, who are actually fairly intuitive and helpful. Make use of them frequently, especially in the early stages of the game as the foundation for your realms is laid down. By following their advice and the tips above, The Powers That Be may bless and keep you so that Ragnarok n' Roll or the Four Surfers of the Apocalypso never trouble your domain.

5

Warcraft II: The Tides of Darkness

80

arcraft II relies heavily on sensible troop and resource management, but this is only part of the equation. Plan on mounting vicious, unrestrained attacks to beat opposing forces. Whether you're playing against the computer or multiplayer, good resource and battle management, and an uninhibited desire to kick butt is the only way to succeed.

STRATEGIES FOR SOLO PLAY

There is one overriding rule in Blizzard Entertainment's *Warcraft II: Tides of Darkness*: use overwhelming force first. This is one game where piecemeal attacks will only make your pieces a meal for your opponent. Above all, don't start a multi-front war; when facing more than one foe, take them out one at a time. Long before magic and flying dragons show up in the game, you can master the essentials of victory by following this brutally simple approach. Indeed, you won't make it to the land of paladins and ogre-magi unless you master the basics of mass warfare first. Keep in mind that—with the exception of spells—virtually everything in *Warcraft II* is the same for either orc or human forces. What works for one will work for the other.

CD-ROM
Check out the CD-ROM included in this book for the demo version of *Warcraft II: Tides of Darkness*.

PATIENCE, PATIENCE

Of course, to get there first with the most, you sometimes have to move last. This seeming paradox results from the overriding importance of mass in *Warcraft II*. In many

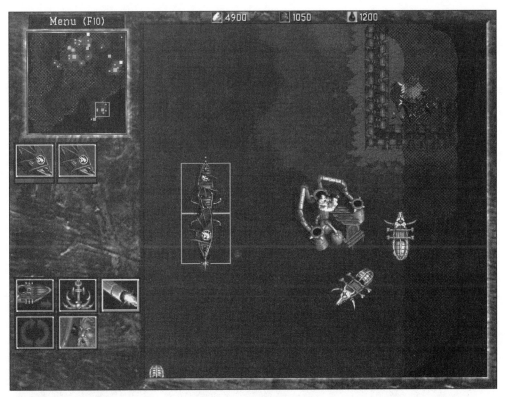

With careful sailing, you can pound the refinery without taking fire from the guard tower. Crafty, that!

scenarios, you will have to build up a force, discover the enemy's hiding place first and then dispatch an expeditionary force to deal with the problem. You will need a solid economic base, a secure rear area, and patience. Patience is truly a virtue; there are no time limits in effect. The Golden Rule is also active: he who has the gold makes the rules. If you are the richest of them all, you usually win. Don't be too aggressive, though; sometimes knowing when not to fight is harder and more important than knowing when to mount an attack.

A solid economy in *Warcraft II* means having enough gold, lumber, and oil to support your operations. Before beginning your five-year plan, however, you need to secure your base area. Build enough troops to provide a screen, and a reaction force to take down any raiding enemies. The computer *will* raid, and it can be humiliating to have your great lumber yard burned down because your elves are off frolicking with

the squirrels on the other side of the map. Don't overdo the garrison; a group of three or four footmen or knights backed up by elves will do the trick at most choke points.

Build an Infrastructure

Your first task, after securing your base, will be to build an infrastructure to support a large number and variety of combat forces. Your first need is gold; all things start with money. Seize every gold mine you find. If possible, build a new hall near any new mines you find; the reduced distance between mine and hall will speed up the accumulation of riches, thus making the whole operation easier to defend.

Remember that your stockpile of resources is equal to the total of all resources your forces gather anywhere on the map. A hall and mine halfway across the map contribute just as much as your original mining operation. If you need to maximize your mining efforts, assign multiple miners to the job. The mine will play out faster, but that money just goes into your hall, where it is probably safer than in the ground anyway. Just be

Over-cutting leads to scarcity; maybe we should have kept the EPA after all?

sure to protect a new hall/mine complex; it is very embarrassing (not to mention fiscally unsound) to invest 1200 gold in a new hall, only to have it burned down around your ears.

Assign your excess worker bees to clear-cutting the forests. You always need some lumber coming in, especially for shipbuilding, but it is usually easy to find. Unlike mining, however, woodcutting has implications beyond the economic. Forests are impassable; as you cut down trees, you clear paths into or through the obstacle. It is quite possible to find yourself suddenly without the wall of trees which had been blocking an orcish assault, because your overzealous lumberjacks hauled away all the redwoods. On the other hand, with careful planning and a bit of patience, you can use the same tactic to cut a path into the enemy's rear areas. In constricted locations, be on the lookout for places where a little selective logging can open up new sites for facilities, but be sure not to give the enemy a clear shot at your heartland in the process.

Oil is essential for naval war, as well as for the higher levels of unit upgrades. Usually you have enough, but you will also have to provide a naval force to protect your oil fields and tankers. Likewise, interdicting the enemy's flow of black gold will pay dividends. The computer's naval patrols are usually not very aggressive, but be careful not to let your roving destroyers lead the bad guys back to your own Persian Gulf. Close patrols can protect your wells, if necessary; against human opponents, such caution will be rewarded.

Building a higher level of hall will make your resource extraction operations more effective. A keep or castle will pay for itself eventually; such structures are necessary for the recruitment of the better sort of units. Defend your halls at all costs, and attack the enemy's if possible. Building your settlements with an outer ring of relatively cheap farms is useful, as the enemy tends to attack Old MacDonald at the expense of more lucrative targets.

BASIC INSTALLATION VALUES

INSTALLATION	GOLD	WOOD	OIL
Farm	500	250	
Barracks	700	450	
Hall	1200	800	
Lumber Mill	600	450	
Blacksmith	800	450	100
Tower	550	200	
Shipyard	800	450	

(Continued on next page)

(Continued from previous page)

INSTALLATION	GOLD	WOOD	OIL
Stables	1000	300	
Church	900	500	
Foundry	700	400	400
Refinery	800	350	200
Inventor	1000	400	

When invading, keep in mind that peasants and peons will not ordinarily fight each other, and it is quite possible to have workers of several parties mining the same gold or chopping in the same forest. Stationing some soldiers around your mines is a good way of keeping the other side out, but be alert. Peons and peasants scurry like ants, and slow moving soldiers often find it hard to kill them faster than a hall can train them. Best to take a catapult or ballista after the hall, and stop the infestation at the source. Likewise, keep enemy artillery away from your vital buildings at all costs.

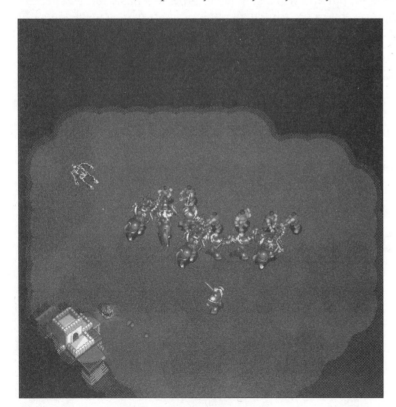

How's this for a fair fight: Knights vs. Peasants.

Begin Your Military Build Up

Economy protected and in high gear, your next task is a military build up. For the most part, quantity is more important than quality—if the quantity is great enough. Until gold is abundant, use hordes of basic foot soldiers and missile troops stiffened with *section leaders* of a higher caliber, like knights and ogres. Eventually you will want to field hordes of better troops like knights and ogres. Footmen and grunts soon become bad bargains, as they cannot equal the power of knights and ogres yet cost nearly as much. Again, lots of gold means fewer compromises. Upgrade when you can, because upgrades make expensive units that much more effective. However you proceed, do not attack until you have a massive force, one that seems large enough to kill the enemy twice over. You can win without such preparations, but the issue will be in doubt. Sending units on raiding parties is generally fruitless, as they are just as likely to die without accomplishing anything as they are to make a dent in the enemy's capabilities.

BASIC UNIT VALUES

UNIT	ARMOR	ATTACK	RANGE	SEE	MOVE	GOLD	WOOD	OIL
Grunt/Footman	2	2-9	1	4	10	600		
Troll/Elf	0	3-9	4	5	10	500	50	
Ogre/Knight	4	2-12	1	4	13	800	100	
Berserker/Ranger	0	3-9	4	6	10	500	50	
Magi/Paladin	4	2-12	1	5	13	800	100	
Catapult/Ballista	0	25-80	8	9	5	900	300	
Destroyer	10	2-35	4	8	5	700	350	700
Battleship/Juggernaut	15	50-130	6	8	3	1000	500	1000

Advance with melee troops in the lead, backed up by missile forces. Axe throwers and archers should stay back just far enough to avoid the fray, yet reach the enemy with their weapons; upgrading range will help here. Missile troops are nearly helpless in melee, so protect them; conversely, seek out enemy missile men with your own close-in fighters.

Protect your artillery, too; while catapults and ballistas can blast enemy troops at a distance, they are also terribly vulnerable and can't fire in close. Upgrade troops when resources permit. Again, lots of gold leads to great armies. Better armor first, followed by attack strength improvements for melee troops, commit damage, and then

The Orcish Phalanx leads the way. Note how missile troops back up grunts, while the artillery sports a heavy guard of its own.

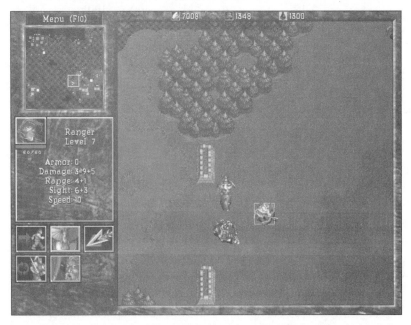

Level 7 Ranger helps guard the gates. Note his cautious location behind the much studlier Paladins.

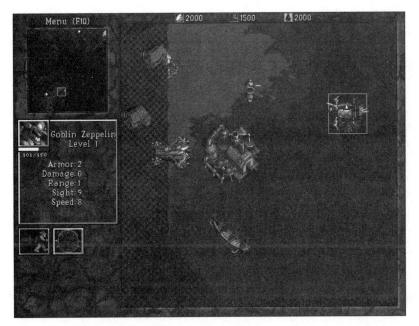

Shore defenses plus naval patrols make this target a tough one. That's why you use aerial reconnaissance before the attack.

range for archers. Build rangers and berserkers as soon as you can, as these upgrades really bring missile troops into their own.

The only purpose of naval warfare is to support the land battle. The same is true of air units, though aerial combat forces arrive rather late in the game. Warships need to clear a path for your transports and tankers, and deny the same to the enemy. Also, shore bombardment is vital to winning several scenarios; upgraded cannons help here, and upgraded armor makes your battleships and juggernauts much more survivable. Don't build ships for the sake of it; have a real use in mind. As for air units, reconnaissance is the task for much of the game; combat units like gryphons and dragons figure prominently in later missions, but you will still win or lose with your ground troops.

That should get you started on the right path, whether orc or human. Remember, attack first, attack with power, and always, always kick an orc when he's down.

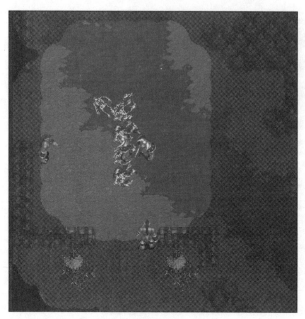

See what happens to raiding parties?

STRATEGIES FOR MULTIPLAYER GAMES

Make sure you know the terms of the battle before you begin!

If you've ever participated in a network gaming session, you already know how much fun multiplayer games can be. You also know how nasty it can get; it goes without saying that human players are better than computer-controlled foes, but along with those improvements come some undesirable elements. Every network gamer has to deal with certain common people and situations: the arrogant winner, the disgruntled loser, or simply the sting of defeat at the hands of a real, live person. For most people, network games entail higher stakes than bouts with the computer. After all, when the computer frags you in an action game or destroys your fantasy empire, it doesn't make fun of you afterwards. Human players do.

The intense competition of network games makes it pretty tough for newcomers to learn the ropes. Often the new guy finds himself trounced before he even gets started, and it's hard to come away with any valuable insight when you've been eliminated before you even get a chance to explore the territory. *Warcraft II* can be particularly nasty in this respect: hordes of mean little guys swarm down upon your defenseless base, shrouded in the Fog of War. You often don't know where they came from or how there got to be so many of them—all you know is you're finished.

No chapter can convey all the subtleties of network *Warcraft II*, but here are a few tips for getting up to speed with your network gaming pals or getting a leg up on your equally talented opponents.

LEARN THE INTERFACE

It is quite common in *Warcraft II* games that an inability to issue precise commands in the heat of battle can cost someone the match. There are several ways to order your *Warcraft II* troops, and you need to find the one that works best for you in tight situations. The old *Warcraft* mouse configuration is good for veterans of that game, while the newer interface is perhaps a bit more streamlined. Keyboard commands are particularly useful because they're so fast. Learn them if you feel comfortable with them. Also get in the habit of issuing commands in the shortest possible fashion. For example, never use the Mine Gold/Chop Trees button. Right-clicking on the forest or gold mine accomplishes the same thing much faster.

PLAY THE SOLO GAME—AND WIN

If you can beat the solo game (either as Orcs or Humans) then you'll go a long way towards mastering multiplayer conflicts. In many games this isn't the case because the computer opponent fails to use the really nasty tactics that human players will always attempt. To some extent this is true in *Warcraft II*. Even on the most difficult levels the computer has a tendency to attack you piecemeal instead of amassing a huge army and crushing you, but the level of opposition in Act IV gets high enough that you'll be forced to improve your game. Solo play will teach you to increase your efficiency and deal with pressure. Those last few missions feature lots of offense by your computer opponents. And because there are no easy-win features (like walling up the computer opponent's base in *Command & Conquer*) you'll have to learn legitimate skills.

Still, always bear in mind that multiplayer games are a different animal than single-player games. Unlike the computer, which likes to keep probing at a single part of your defenses, humans use distraction and guerrilla attacks. And unlike the computer, humans are indeed capable of producing huge strike forces, so be prepared.

UNDERSTAND THE MAP

Before you even start to play, you should have some clues about your strategy. How's that? Well, for starters, look at the size of the map you'll be fighting on, and the number of players in the game. Don't let the master player breeze past this stuff; make sure he tells you what map you're playing on and what size it is. If he knows these things and you don't, he has a huge advantage.

Let's say you're on a small (32×32) map designed for four players, but you're only playing a two-player game. Among other things, you can now deduce that:

- There are four start positions on the map, probably one in each of the map's four corners, and your opponent could be in any one of them. Plan accordingly.

- There is limited room on the map, so start making cheap troops early for defense, or else you could be knocked out by a small scouting party.

- There are almost definitely two free gold mines out there; they were supposed to be for those extra two players. Because only two people are playing the game, they're unattended. You'd better go look for them and mine them, quick!

Your strategy would be somewhat different for a large map: long-term growth would be more important. So make sure you know the terms of the battle before you begin!

EXPLORE AS FAST AS POSSIBLE

Knowledge is power, and you need all the power you can get. Fog of War cuts down somewhat on the value of reconnaissance, but it's still critical to know where important resources like gold mines and oil patches are. If you've uncovered the whole map and can see the big picture, then you'll be able to predict what your enemies are doing just by knowing where they started and where the important goodies are. Use a Peon or a Grunt to scout the land if you don't have a Balloon or an expendable Destroyer. They aren't fast, but if you're lucky they'll survive for a while and give you valuable information.

One thing you should try to figure out right from the start is what terrain dominates the landscape, and which resources (if any) are rare. This way you will avoid

Dashing down to find an unattended gold mine.

building a useless fleet of ships in a pond, or building lots of Archers and Ballistas on a map where lumber is scarce.

EXPAND LIKE CRAZY

This may be obvious, but there are a few caveats, especially if you're used to single-player *Warcraft II*. In the single-player game, you'll find that speedy expansion isn't critical until the last few missions, where the computer tends to eat up gold very quickly. In single-player games it's often best to expand slowly so you can consolidate your new territory. In multiplayer games everyone's expanding as fast as they can, and by concentrating on fortifying your base or mining only the closest gold mines, you will end up losing out on the up-for-grabs resources. Your window of opportunity shrinks at an alarming rate, so start sending out Peons as soon as possible.

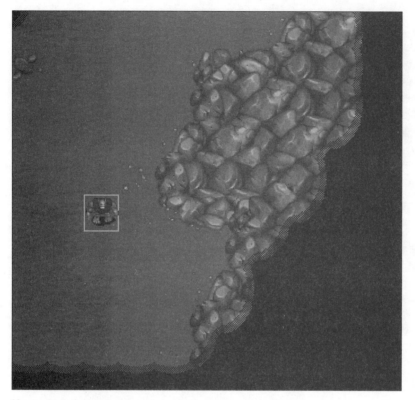

If you don't have aerial units, a spare Peon can explore.

Single Peons, or Peons with a single-unit escort, are a great way to take over new mines in network sessions. Send them out, and when they find an unoccupied mine, have them build a town hall right next to the mine. Then start getting gold as fast as possible! Some of your Peons will be killed as they explore, and some of your halls will be destroyed, but this early, unprotected expansion is vital. If just one or two of these new outposts lasts a few minutes unmolested, build a few Barracks and Cannon Towers nearby and start to fortify the area. This leads us to the next tip.

MAKE MULTIPLE BARRACKS OR SHIP YARDS

Beginning players mistakenly think of each battle solely in terms of getting *more* resources and producing *more* units than the other guys. Not so! Games are usually determined by who gets resources *faster* and produces military units *faster* than their opponents. It may seem wasteful to build four Barracks at a key site—after all, that's

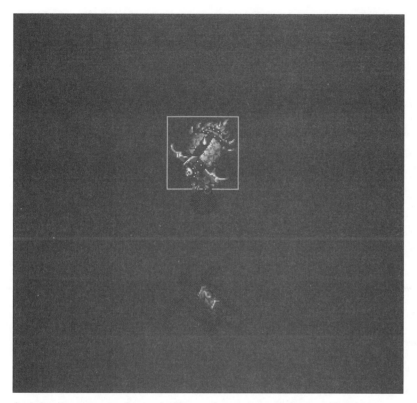

Aerial units are great for exploring, and can spot submarines like this one.

gold you could be spending to make new units—but after getting swamped a few times you'll find that the ability to produce new combat units quickly outweighs the inefficiency of having several buildings that all do the exact same thing.

Multiple barracks allow you to be flexible. Instead of having a huge standing army that could easily be in the wrong place at the wrong time, you can have relatively small defense forces and augment them quickly when necessary. In scenarios where ships are key, the same rule apples: make lots of shipyards, or else your main base can easily be swamped by a big invasion fleet and your exiting shipyards will promptly be destroyed. Game over.

WATCH AND LEARN

Obviously there are hundreds of specific situations that cannot be covered in a single chapter, but here's a great tip that will help you in any situation. After you have been

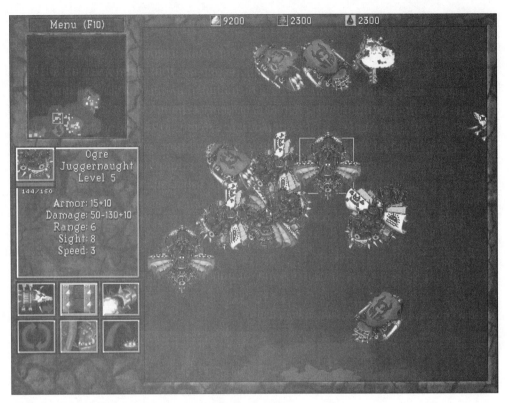

Multiple Shipyards or Barracks will often save your life.

beaten, ask the winner how he won, or what he thinks you did wrong. If he isn't a jerk, he will probably give you an honest answer. However, even the most honest player is sometimes reluctant to reveal his best tips, so if at all possible you should *watch* a good player during a multiplayer game. Analyze what he's doing and how it differs from your general strategy. In the heat of battle, players forget they're being watched, and they won't hold back any secrets. That's why this is the absolute best way to learn. If you want even more insights, try to watch several sides of a network game: go back and forth between computers and make a note of what everyone's doing. You'll get a real sense of what's going on in the total game, and what conditions or tactics resulted in one player's victory and another player's defeat.

A big fleet of Juggernauts doesn't hurt either.

BUILDING NEW WORLDS WITH THE *WARCRAFT II* SCENARIO EDITOR

Thanks to its great networking capabilities, *Warcraft II* is a game with strong replay value. However, after playing through all the standard maps provided with the game, you might find that your games are getting more and more predictable. Enter the built-in scenario editor; it's an excellent way to increase *Warcraft II*'s life-span on your hard drive. Many players avoid using scenario editors because they tend to be awkward or difficult to use, and in single-player games they're of little value unless you enjoy designing levels for your friends. *Warcraft II*'s scenario editor, however, is quick and easy to use—and there's a real benefit to creating new scenarios. Instead of constantly fighting over

the same old piece of land, your multiplayer games can now take place in new and unexplored territories.

One of the hardest things about creating a scenario is figuring out what order to do things in. Should you build the map first? Adjust player variables? If these problems aren't resolved quickly, they lead to frustration and half-finished scenarios. This section will outline the ten-step process you can use to create my scenario, *Implosion*. Follow these steps when you make your own *Warcraft II* scenarios, and you'll find that things progress much more smoothly when you aren't always worrying about what to do next.

1. PICK A THEME

Bob Ross, an artist who used to do oil paintings on TV, was able to create a beautiful picture in just half an hour. He seemingly composed his paintings on-the-fly, making things up as he went along. You might be tempted to use the same approach when you make a *Warcraft II* scenario, but having a clear idea of what you want before you start to work is much more practical and strongly recommend.

For *Implosion*, the designer definitely wants a quick scenario—something that won't last for hours on end. All four players will start out with a fair number of Orc units and a very small gold mine. The center of the map will contain a gold mine with almost unlimited capacity. Hence the players will all strive to control the center mine, and create the implosion of the scenario's title. A strong but passive computer-controlled force will defend the central gold mine, adding an element of complexity to the scenario. Any player who wastes all his troops attacking the computer will be too weak to hold off the other players; but if all the human players just sit around and wait for the others to attack the computer, nothing will happen. The result is a scenario where players must carefully gauge how many troops they're willing to waste in an attack on the central gold mine.

2. ADJUST MAP, PLAYER, AND STARTING PROPERTIES

With your theme in mind, pick a large map with the Wasteland tile set—a large map to accommodate four players and Wasteland simply because the look of it appealed to this designer.

Now adjust the Player Properties menu. Players 1 through 4 are human-controlled Orcs, while Player 5 is a computer-controlled Human force (confusing isn't it?) The AI

(Artificial Intelligence) settings for players 1 through 4 are meaningless, since humans will control those forces. Player 5 gets a Passive AI, which simply means that the computer will sit there and defend its territory, never building new units or moving from the spot. This is important because with an active AI the computer would build a vast army with its endless supply of gold and the humans wouldn't stand a chance!

For Starting Properties, give all four players 10,000 gold; 10,000 oil; and 5,000 wood. This allows everyone to quickly build any desired structures and fortify their armies.

3. CHANGE UNIT PROPERTIES AND UPGRADE PROPERTIES, IF DESIRED

Do not change Unit or Upgrade Properties for this scenario. If you like to play with these variables, go right ahead—just make sure the people who are playing your scenario understand that you've tinkered with these values. This is especially true if you're

Each player starts with a small army and the farms to support it.

playing along with your friends. Just imagine what would happen if, unbeknownst to your pals, you'd made Peons the strongest military unit in the game! Many of them would fail to notice this change, and be amazed when you bowl 'em over with your thirty-Peon army. Actually, they'd only be amazed for a moment, and then they'd be ticked off.

4. SKETCH IN THE LAND, WATER, MOUNTAINS, AND PLAYER START POSITIONS

The map starts as a big, unadorned square of land. With the largest brush size, sketch in the major water bodies and mountain ranges. There are two great reasons to use these large brushes. First, the obvious: creating the map takes less time when you use big brushes. Just as you wouldn't want to paint your house with a watercolor brush, you definitely don't want to create an ocean square by square.

Also, big brushes let you maintain your sense of proportion. You can build major landscape features quickly, watching the mini-map all the while, and correct errors just as quickly if the map gets out of proportion. If you choose to concentrate on a small area instead, you can easily lose sight of how it fits into the map as a whole. So paint the map with broad strokes and worry about the details later.

The easiest way to ensure that everyone gets a fair deal is to make the map roughly symmetrical, and start every player out in a similar area. This can lead to boredom, but asymmetrical maps often grant an advantage to one player over another, so they require much more play testing.

Player Properties				
Player	Race	Controller	A.I. Players	
1 (Red):	⊙ Human ⊙ Orc	Human ▾	Land Attack ▾	OK
2 (Blue):	⊙ Human ⊙ Orc	Human ▾	Land Attack ▾	Cancel
3 (Green):	⊙ Human ⊙ Orc	Human ▾	Land Attack ▾	Help
4 (Violet):	⊙ Human ⊙ Orc	Human ▾	Land Attack ▾	
5 (Orange):	⊙ Human ⊙ Orc	Computer ▾	Passive ▾	
6 (Black):	⊙ Human ⊙ Orc	Human ▾	Land Attack ▾	
7 (White):	⊙ Human ⊙ Orc	Human ▾	Land Attack ▾	
8 (Yellow):	⊙ Human ⊙ Orc	Human ▾	Land Attack ▾	

Here are the Player Properties.

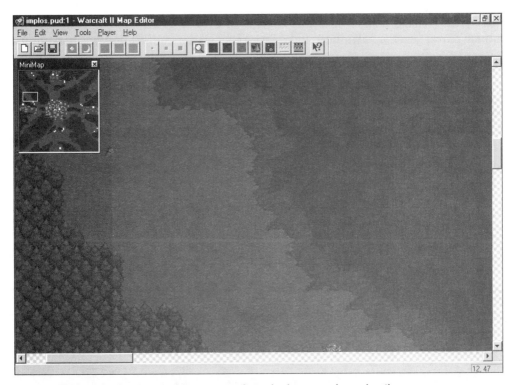

Sketch in the major land and water masses first—don't worry about details.

5. ADD TREES AND OIL

Trees are both an obstacle and a resource, so be careful about where you place them. Too many trees can limit a player's growth, but too few can be crippling as well. Just make sure that every player has roughly equal access to trees. If players don't have equal access to trees, the player with fewer trees must have some sort of compensating resource.

Oil can be critical or superfluous, depending on the sort of map you're building. In *Implosion* there isn't much water, so oil is pretty useless; but it was added nevertheless. If someone *really* wants to build boats, why should the designer stop them?

6. ADD GOLD MINES

Gold mines are the single most important resource in the game. Nothing gets done without gold! Therefore you should be very careful about where you put those mines,

and how much gold is in each of them. For *Implosion*, this is an easy matter: each human player gets a small mine with 17,500 gold, and the central mine gets maximum gold (637,500).

7. ADD UNITS

Now it's time to add units. By giving players a lot of starting units and very little gold, you can force them to adapt to their situation and work with what they have. By giving them lots of resources but very few starting units, you give them more of a chance to implement their own plans. And remember: if you don't give a player at least one Peon or Great Hall, he cannot build any new structures!

Many scenarios give each player only one Peon to start with. This results in a slow, expansion-oriented game. *Implosion* gives each of the humans a small army to start with, and enough gold and lumber to make construction easy. This keeps the scenario quick.

Note that passive computer players won't build their own units, so you have to place them all yourself. Active computer players (with the Land, Air, or Sea attack AI) will create their own units, so all they really need to start with is a Peon. If you give

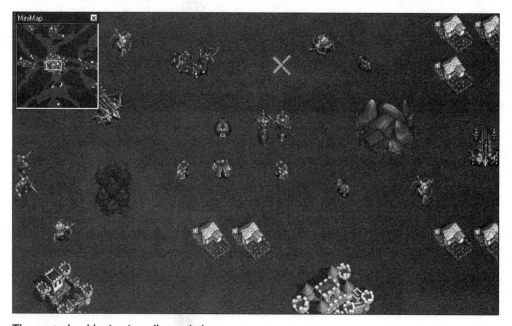

The central gold mine is well guarded.

an active computer player too many units to start with, it can make life rough on the human players.

8. ADD STRUCTURES

Most players like to position their own buildings, so in most scenarios consider not pre-placing too many structures. However, some scenarios—especially ones in which one player starts out in an entrenched position—demand that you pre-place certain buildings. In *Implosion* only buildings for the passive computer player were pre-placed.

9. PRETTY UP THE MAP

Now that you've got all the essentials in place, you should make the map look good. Use smaller brushes to work out blocky parts of the landscape; play with the Light/Dark buttons to add shadows to land and water; use the Filler brush setting to place debris and pockmarks on the ground; and add Critters to roam around and liven up the place. Do as much or as little as you wish.

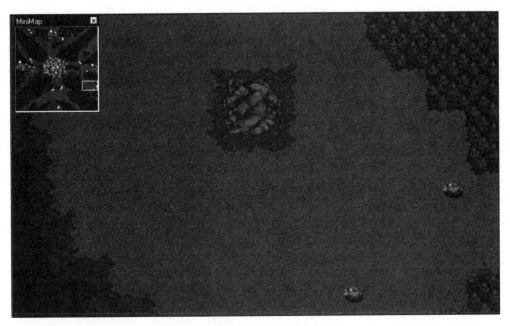

The critters in the corner add life to the map.

10. PLAY TEST IT!

Test your scenario with a highly critical eye. Try to make all aspects of your scenario bulletproof. *Implosion* should work pretty well for which it was intended: a fast, bloody game filled with intrigue and calculation. *Implosion* (IMPLOS.PUD) can be found on your CD in the WAR2 folder, along with a 2-player variant named IMP2P.PUD. Try 'em out and see what you think. Perhaps you'll like them—or perhaps you'll just be relieved that I'm not a full-time game designer.

6

Settlers II

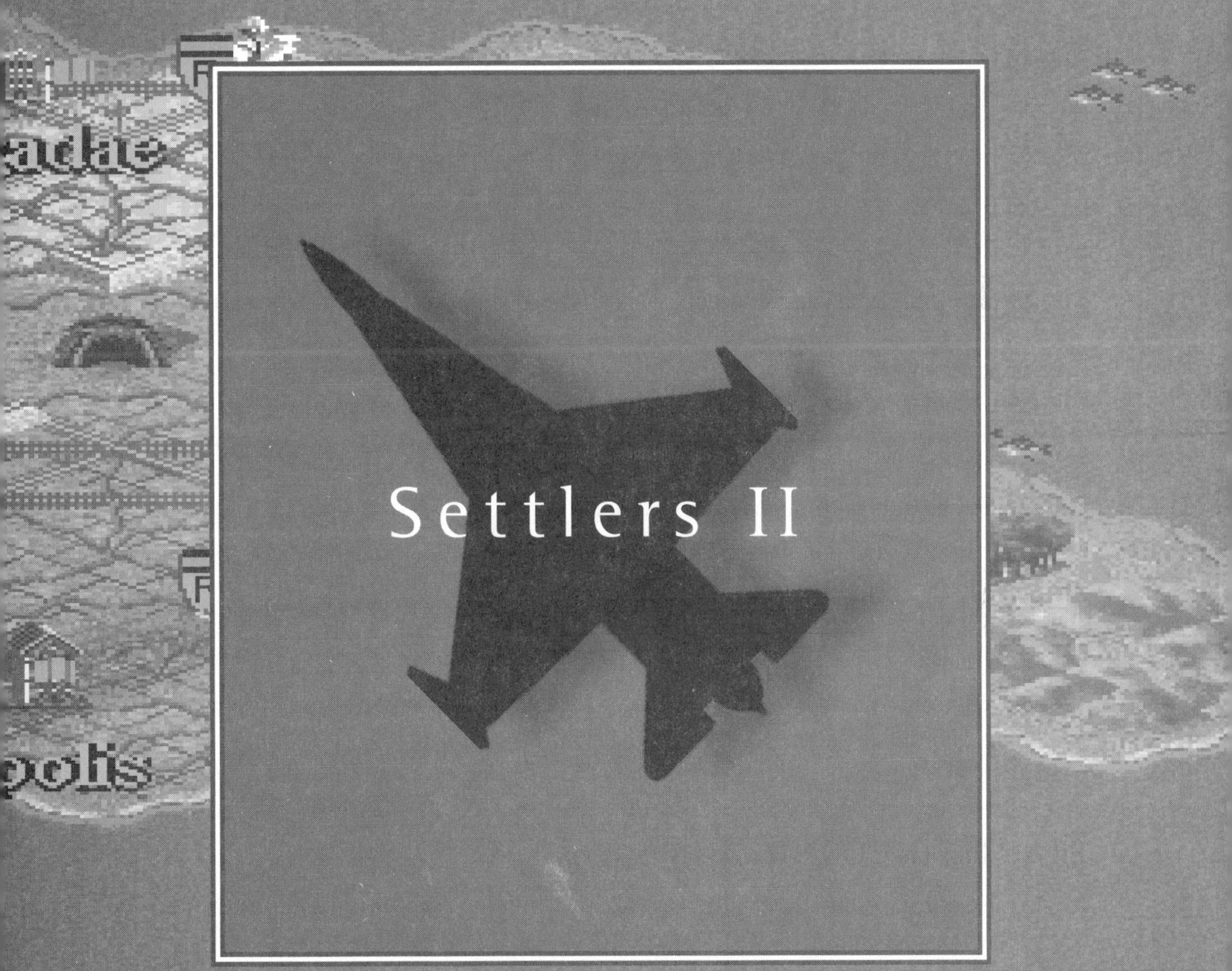

Settlers II by Blue Byte can be a fascinating game, but also a frustrating game, largely because the control you exert over your settlers is so indirect. It's fascinating because you can watch your civilization grow and flourish, each little settler performing his tasks with little or no guidance from you. But it's frustrating when you'd like to affect the game more directly, marching settlers here and there instead of controlling them through subtler actions.

SETTING THE SETTLERS STRAIGHT

The key techniques for improving your control over your civilization, both in economic and military terms, will be discussed in the following sections, along with a variety of other hints and tips, including a means of speeding up the game.

STARTING ECONOMIES

In the early stages of your civilization, all your buildings will be quite close together, so the only real concern is which structures to build. First build a woodcutter next to a suitable bunch of trees and a quarry next to a pile of rock outcrops. Build a forester right next to the woodcutter, to replenish the supply of trees, but *turn off* the forester's production (with the red X) immediately after it has been built. If you don't do this, you'll find the center

CD-ROM
Check out the CD-ROM included in this book for the demo version of *Settlers II*.

All you need to start with are a few basic structures, like a woodcutter and quarry.

of your civilization so crammed with trees that you can't build any new structures. Only re-activate the forester when the tree supply is getting low.

Also build a well, a sawmill right next to the woodcutter, and a fishery if water is convenient. The fishery will build up a decent supply of food for later mining operations. Hunters' lodges are generally not worth building, as the supply of game tends to run out faster than the supply of fish. Finally, you should build a farm if you can find a suitable area with *lots* of open space around it. This completes the first phase of your settlement.

EXPANSION AND CONSOLIDATION

After these bare necessities have been established, it's time to acquire the remaining supplies you'll need for a successful civilization. You should also be expanding in this phase, at least until you run into your neighbors.

Use the space bar frequently to determine what sites are best for building.

Build barracks at the fringes of your settlements to expand your borders. Build guardhouses instead of barracks when you know you'll be approaching an enemy border. Watchtowers should only be built when dealing with a potentially deadly foe, and fortresses are generally not necessary, except in the grandest of wars.

During this expansion you'll probably find some mountainous terrain; send geologists to determine what resources can be found there. You need to build gold, iron, and coal mines during this stage if possible; granite mines generally aren't needed if you have granite bluffs for your quarries.

Once the mines are established, you should add a mill and bakery next to your farm (but not so close that they impinge on the fields). These buildings will help produce bread, which greatly speeds your miners' efforts. Also build a brewery if you have discovered enemy nations, as a brewery is necessary if you're to create more soldiers. More on this later.

As near to the mines as possible, build a mint and an iron smelter. Then make a metalworks if you're low on tools and an armory if you've discovered any other civilizations. The metalworks is not needed if you have sufficient tools; check the game manual's listing of buildings for which tools are required at which structures. If you do indeed make a metalworks, you should always use the Tools window to adjust which tools are most likely to be produced. Don't be shy—increase the sliding bars of the tools you want to the maximum and drop the others to nearly the minimum.

EXTRA STRUCTURES

You do not need to build a donkey breeder, pig farm, or slaughterhouse. The pig farm/slaughterhouse combination adds more food to your mining efforts, while the donkeys speed up transportation—but you can ignore both in a pinch. Similarly, do not build naval buildings (shipyards and harbor buildings) or storehouses unless you really need to. Some scenarios require ships and storage, while others, especially the early ones, do not.

You should always try to build two or more extra farms, however, as this will increase bread and beer supplies. If you intend to build a pig farm or donkey breeder, then extra farms are absolutely vital; the grain gets spread pretty thinly between the brewery, bakery, donkey breeder, and pig farmer. An extra mill is needed if you have four or more farms.

WARFARE

First, it's vital to understand how soldiers are made. Here's the equation:

1 Helper + 1 Sword + 1 Shield + 1 Beer = 1 Soldier

Helpers are the little guys that run back and forth on roads. You'll almost always have a surplus of them in your headquarters, so they aren't a problem. The trick is getting an armory to churn out swords and shields and a brewery to churn out beer. Get all these items together in your headquarters at once, and turn up the recruitment rate (the first sliding bar under the Military menu) and you'll have soldiers aplenty.

Gold is critical if you want a good army. Soldiers become better if they have a good supply of gold flowing into their barracks. You can control the flow of gold coins to each military building by checking or unchecking the gold coin icon. It's generally sensible to turn off the flow of gold in the interior of your realm, as it's an area your enemies will hopefully never reach. To compensate for this lack of training, increase the

Increase your recruitment rate to the maximum.

second sliding bar under the Military menu, which allows your stronger soldiers to rush to the defense of any building that's come under attack.

Waging war is essentially a matter of gold regulation. First you build a military structure next to your enemy's border, and allow gold to go there (i.e., don't turn off the gold coin button). This will attract any free soldiers that are sitting around in your headquarters. Note that *free soldiers* are any soldiers that are not already posted to a military building and are not actively defending headquarters. (Remember, you can adjust how many soldiers defend headquarters with a menu reached by clicking on headquarters itself.) If you reduce the number of soldiers defending headquarters, the surplus men will leave headquarters for any under-staffed military structures. Don't leave your headquarters undefended, though!

If you have problems getting enough soldiers to man your border outposts, then be sure that you are producing enough beer, swords, and shields to create new ones. Also make sure that your recruitment level under the Military menu is at maximum.

Once your border outpost has enough soldiers, mount an attack on the enemy's nearest military building. Use your strongest soldiers if it's a big target, and use weaker

Cut off supplies of gold to barracks in the middle of your realm.

ones if you've got soldiers to spare and you're attacking a small building. (You can adjust what type of soldiers will attack with a button on the attack menu itself.)

Once your men have taken over the enemy outpost, it becomes yours. Because soldiers are generally scarce and you'll want to continue your expansion, immediately *turn off the gold supply* to the building you mounted your attack from, and *let the gold supply continue* to the building you've just taken over. This way, soldiers from headquarters will march directly into the newly conquered outpost instead of filling up the old one, which is now well behind the front lines and hence doesn't need as many soldiers.

This is the key to successful conquest: always cut off the gold supply to your interior military structures, thus directing soldiers to fill up the outposts on the edge of your realm. As your borders expand, keep turning off the gold supply to buildings that are no longer on the cutting edge of your attack. Ideally you'd have enough soldiers to fully man all of your buildings, not just the border outposts, but in reality you seldom have that luxury.

Catapults are an excellent alternative to all-out attacks, especially when you don't have the manpower to overwhelm an enemy building. Catapult hits gradually reduce the number of soldiers who can occupy an enemy building, eventually destroying it if allowed to attack unchecked. However, catapults become useless once you've taken over or destroyed all enemy buildings within a short radius. Therefore, only build them next to large enemy structures like towers and fortresses that you can't handle by conventional means. This reduces the enemy's ability to attack your borders with large numbers of troops. Catapults also can be used when you'd like to take over a large enemy structure but cannot do it without reducing the manpower inside it first.

OF ROADS AND SPEED

Don't be afraid to dig up roads that are not productive! Keep digging up and re-building roads to your best advantage as you create new buildings: it's free and instant, so there's no reason not to continually move them until you attain the most direct supply routes possible.

One common complaint with *Settlers II* is the lack of speed. The game can drag in the middle to later stages as you wait for resources or soldiers to build up. Never fear! There's a poorly documented key that speeds up the game. Press V to enter double-speed mode, and the game will move along at a significantly faster clip. Press it again to return to normal speed. For those who really have a need for speed, type **thunder** during normal game play and an exclamation point will appear in the top right corner of the screen. Now press and hold the Alt key, and simultaneously press a number between 1 and 6. Depending on which number you choose, you can set the game at normal speed (1), double speed (2), or anything all the way up to six-speed (6). As an added benefit, pressing the F7 key while in Thunder mode will reveal the entire world map.

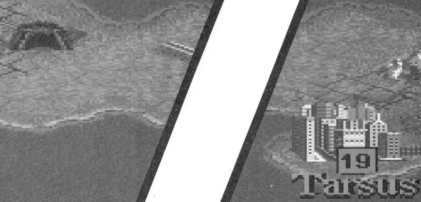

7

Close
Combat

U se history as your guide when you assume either side of the Normandy conflict in this role-playing game of strategy. Today's gamers can experience those 43 historic days from a commander's point of view.

AMERICAN TACTICS

The Normandy campaign wasn't really something the Allied planners anticipated. The month spent in the hedgerows and marshes of the Norman countryside came about because German resistance was tougher than expected and Allied progress correspondingly slower. The result was some 60,000 Allied casualties and a brutal initiation in the horrors of infantry warfare for many inexperienced soldiers.

Microsoft's *Close Combat*, the brainchild of Keith Zabalaoui's Atomic Games, allows you to lead the men of the American 29th Infantry Division through this French hecatomb, or, alternately, to take the role of the experienced German *soldaten* in an attempt to at least delay the by now inevitable collapse of the *Thousand Year Reich*. Here we'll examine what it takes to do the former: lead the Americans to St.-Lô in 43 days or less.

To win the campaign as the Americans, you have to understand what it is you are trying to do. You will eventually take St.-Lô, but time and casualties are the difference between victory and defeat. Do it in less than the historical 43 days, and you're a winner; take more time, or lose too many men, and it's back to basic training.

You accelerate your advance by winning battles and slow down when you lose. The better you do, the more battles you skip ahead; winning big moves your timetable up considerably, but losing slows you down so you have to fight again over familiar terrain.

CD-ROM
Check out the CD-ROM included in this book for the demo version of *Close Combat*.

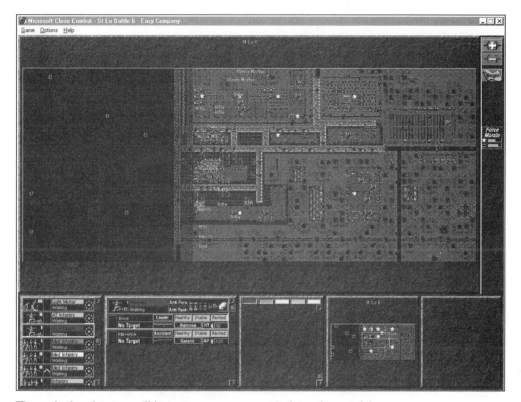

Those depleted teams will become a constant reminder to be careful.

Casualties hurt in several ways; the more replacements you have to take, the more time you'll lose, and too many letters home will hurt your performance rating. The essence of victory, then, is winning fast and efficiently.

WIN FAST AND EFFICIENTLY

Speed and efficiency aren't easy, however. This is first and foremost a command game, not a counter pushing exercise. You take the role of the on-map commander, and it's up to you to lead your men. A foolish order often results in one of two things: your men ignore it, or worse, they follow it and die. Not surprisingly, many of your soldiers are in no hurry to find out if there really is life after death, and while heroism isn't uncommon, you can't depend on a platoon from Sgt. Rock's Easy Company to bail you out of sticky situations.

Speed usually means taking risks, and that doesn't help your efficiency, yet efficiency (in terms of lives) usually means taking it slow and easy, and that doesn't help your speed. While there isn't really a time limit in the individual battles, if you move too slowly you're likely to wind up with less of a victory than you hoped for, as the computer will decide that one or both sides is exhausted after a certain amount of strenuous (and bloody) activity.

The upshot of all this is that you need to prosecute your attacks rapidly and use all of your forces to the utmost, while keeping casualties down.

SETTING UP THE ASSAULT

The way to start a battle is by re-deploying your forces to locations supporting your own plan of attack. You should focus on killing the enemy, and forcing a withdrawal, not on merely capturing victory point locations. Many of the VP spots will be smack in the middle of killing grounds, so a headlong rush to glory will soon become the fast track to a white cross and a telegram to Ma and Pa in Peoria. On the other hand, if you force Hitler's legions to goose-step in the opposite direction, you'll take all those VP locations *gratis* when the Germans pull back.

The terrain you should be interested in is that which either shields you from enemy fire or allows you to fire more effectively on the enemy. Command this sort of ground, and the other locations will follow. Holding the hedgerow line or stone house that commands a VP spot 100 meters away is often far better than bull rushing the objective itself.

When setting up, anticipate where the Germans will be. Your foes like to line up behind hedgerows, or snipe from farm houses. Position your forces to put maximum firepower on those locations. This doesn't necessarily mean clumping your men together; that isn't too smart, what with German assault guns roaming the fields in front of you and 8cm mortars raining good Ruhr steel on your pointed little heads.

Keep in mind that the map in *Close Combat* is very small in real world measurements. If you have a line of sight to it, you can hit it. You should have a base of heavy firepower, machine guns, BARs, or armor to support every advance. Even your rifle teams, with their semi-auto Garands, can lay down some awesome fire, so position your supporting forces so that their fire converges, but their physical locations diverge.

When you finally assault a position, you can bring your teams together as they cross no-man's land, coming to a sharp and concentrated point at the objective.

Of course, assaults are dicey. The best way to take a hedgerow or house is to blast the occupants before you close with them. Barring that, use smoke to cover your advance, supported by heavy suppressive fire. A good rule of thumb is to use three

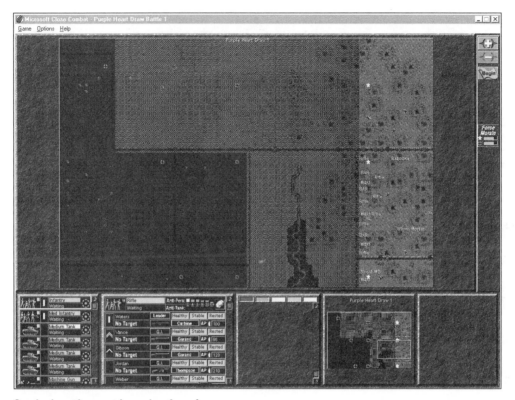

Smoke 'em if ya got 'em, dog faces!

teams for an assault. One large team can advance under smoke, while two others provide fire support. Try using machine gun fire from the flanks as well. Mortars are fine for disrupting and suppressing defenders behind walls and hedgerows, but aren't too useful for dislodging Germans from buildings and bunkers. They are great, however, for laying down smoke screens; just keep an eye on your ammo count.

Direct fire artillery, in the form of anti-tank guns, can be effective in blasting dug-in Germans, but you should do so from a safe distance (keep this in mind when you deploy). Recon teams have good close-in firepower with their SMGs but little range; use them to scout and to ambush Germans at close range. Recon teams are usually too small for assaults.

And of course, there are tanks. Tanks and tank destroyers are your mobile artillery. Unfortunately, the Germans come equipped with lots of anti-armor weapons, which can kill your vehicles from a distance. This is particularly true with your ubiquitous M3 half-tracks, which are really little more than armored machine guns. Don't

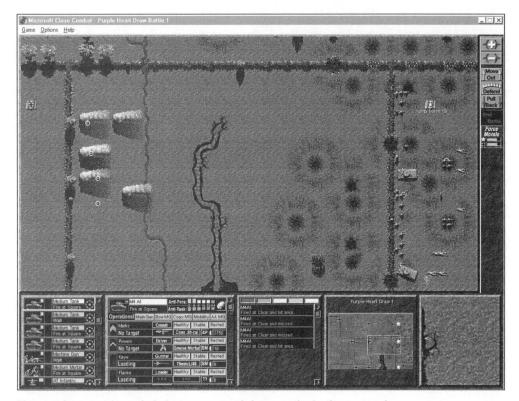

Heavy infantry with satchel charges are cool, but you don't always get them.

succumb to the temptation to rush your armor up to the hedgerows and blast away at point-blank range; a Panzerfaust will ruin your day, for sure. Instead, sit your armor back a bit, behind cover, and lob HE and MG fire at your enemies.

In an advance, scout with infantry first, to locate AT positions and enemy armor. Then, maneuver your own AT teams and your tanks to knock out German vehicles, and use your mortars to suppress AT guns. Tanks are too valuable to waste. They are often the difference between dislodging a pesky MG 42 team and routing from battle. You have to balance caution and aggression here; you need that fire support, but losing a tank hurts morale, and often leaves you with too little firepower to do the job.

EXECUTING THE ASSAULT

So, how do you get to grips with Fritz? Use the hedgerows and buildings for cover, and don't march up the roads. Nothing ruins your day like an assault gun decimating your teams from 150 meters away as they stroll down a country lane. Save infantry smoke for the final assault, where you'll need to cross those last few meters of open ground. Use mortar and vehicle smoke to cover strategic moves.

Many battles will see you facing the Germans over a hedged field, with both sides lined up in the hedgerows on opposite sides. Your superior rifle firepower can often force the Germans to move away, but you will face more machine gun fire than you dreamed possible, so use mortars and artillery if you have it to even the odds. Once the Reich Rats begin to flee, you can pop smoke and advance in bounds. If possible, out flank the entire enemy position by using the north or south map edge as cover.

Keep moving forward, even if only slowly. Once you falter, convincing your troops to move again gets tough. VP spots are good to get, in case the battle ends with both of you exhausted, but killing Germans is the way to win. The Germans will withdraw if you hurt them too much, as they can't sustain the kind of casualties you can.

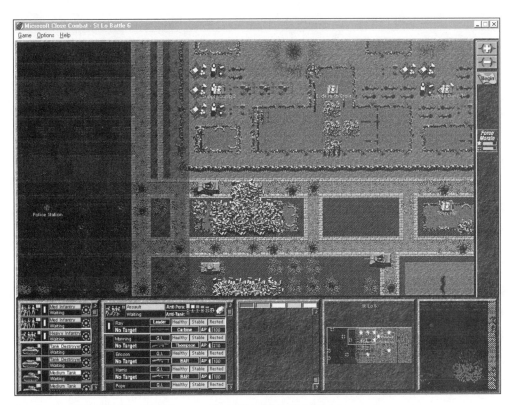

Smoke can help shield your Shermans from the 88 in the bunker.

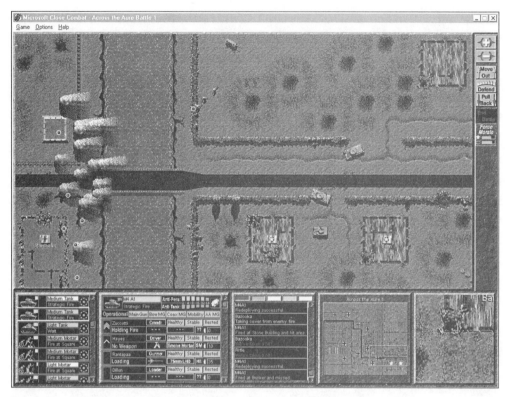

Try overloading one flank; that open northern expanse is a killing field.

If you walk into a killing zone, try to move laterally to cover, and regroup and try again. Don't brazen it out with inferior firepower, but return from a different angle with more muscle. You can't win by out-finessing the Germans, you have to out-muscle them, so don't be afraid to use excessive force; all of France is a free fire zone, and you've got the Ronson to make it burn.

GERMAN TACTICS TO HOLD BACK THE TWILIGHT OF THE REICH

As the Germans in *Close Combat* you are outnumbered, outgunned, and in a hopeless strategic position. No matter how well you fight, the Americans will eventually take St.-Lô. Your job is to make this task as lengthy and costly as possible.

You have several advantages over your foes, so use them. Your troops are better trained and more experienced than the GIs. You have more machine guns, better anti-tank weapons, and usually have the advantage in close-in fighting, due to your discipline and training. Most of all, you have the terrain of Normandy on your side. The hedgerows and farms of this part of France give you the chance to turn Eisenhower's Great Crusade into a funeral procession. To win, you'll have to ensure that the road to St.-Lô is the American infantry's march to Golgotha.

CONSERVATION OF FORCE

Of course, the way *Close Combat* works, the better you do, the less support you get, so success can sometimes mean you have to do even more with less. If you win consistently, you'll never see the best armor, and mortars and heavy infantry will be scarce.

Conservation of your force is thus a primary responsibility, second only to killing Americans. Leave the last stand heroics to the fanatics in the SS; you want to preserve not only the honor of the *Wehrmacht* but its soldiers as well. Kill enough GIs and they'll retreat, giving up any victory point (VP) locations they've taken. Do this two or three times in a row and you'll hold up their advance significantly, and still have the ability to strike back in the next series of battles.

Be particularly chary of risking your assault guns and machine gun teams. These two systems will without a doubt kill more of the enemy than all the rest of your troops combined. Luckily, the American AT teams with bazookas aren't terribly effective, though their tanks are deadly at the short ranges prominent in *bocage* fighting. Use the long range of your MG 42s to lay down withering fires from safer distances, and use hedgerows to screen your armor.

Unlike your opponent, you will have many more opportunities to trundle your armor up to the enemy and blast away at point-blank range. Once you've dispatched the Shermans, the bazookas become much less of a threat.

More problematic are the American infantry teams. These are numerous, and well armed, more than a match for your rifle teams without machine gun backup. Massed fire from the American semiautomatic rifles and BARs can decimate your thin lines. Use your MGs and assault guns to kill as many Americans as you can, at as long ranges as possible. Save your rifle and scout teams (with their MP-40 SMGs) for close assaults and ambushes.

Unfortunately, mortars are too often in short supply, so the only HE support you'll get is from armor or AT guns. Never put your AT guns in exposed positions, or too close to the enemy. Put them behind hedgerows, in stone buildings or bunkers, with

Ah, an assault group in ambush—but that gully could get hot real soon.

good lines of fire but well away from the enemy. Ranges are deceptively short in *Close Combat*; a gun halfway across the map is still only a few hundred meters from the enemy. If the GIs get too close to your troops, they can pop smoke and run away, but your gun crews are stuck, so don't let the enemy get that close.

One good rule to follow is to never expose anyone who isn't killing the enemy. If your AT teams don't have any good targets, pull them back. If your SMG teams can't hit the enemy, send them to the flanks, or back to the second line of defense. You don't have enough men to overcome the attacker's numbers in a straight up fight, so don't try to match the Americans man-for-man.

Your machine guns make up for a lot of deficiencies, but one casualty and even an experienced three-man team will get shaky. Pulling back under fire isn't easy, so positioning is important. You have the range, so pick positions with good fields of fire and covered withdrawal possibilities.

Close Combat   **Debriefing**

Victory: Germans

This battle was a decisive German victory!
Americans gained some ground.

Score Summary for American Army						Score Summary for German Army					
	Infantry	Armor	Artillery	Trucks	Terrain		Infantry	Armor	Artillery	Trucks	Terrain
KIA/WIA:	1	0	0	0	---	KIA/WIA:	63	2	0	0	---
Captured:	0	0	0	0	7	Captured:	0	0	0	0	12
Points:	3	0	0	0	5	Points:	126	40	0	0	80

8	Total American Points		Details		Total German Points	246

Infantry Assault Badge
Total Awarded: 4

Off the Beach	Hedgerows!		Hill 192	Top bar = Historical date
2 Days	20 Days	July 1	1 Day	Bottom bar = Game date

June 6	3 Days	Game Score: 203 hours	1 Day	3 Days	August 1
Across the Aure		Game Date: Jul 29, 1944	Purple Heart Draw	St. Lo	6 June thru 4 August, 1944

Command Screen	News Reel	Save Replay	Play Next Battle

A 63:1 kill ratio is what you should be looking for.

Your rifle teams aren't as good as the Americans in laying down fire, but are ideal for supporting the MGs; that's what the *Wehrmacht* did in the war, and you should follow suit. In fact, you could say that the German commander's main job is helping the machine guns do the killing. Luckily for you, the Americans don't get that many MG teams.

Unfortunately, the Americans *do* get tanks, and usually several. Killing Shermans is a top priority. Tanks left free to roam around at will *will* massacre your infantry, so scatter a few AT teams among your machine gunners and riflemen. Maneuver your assault guns (or tanks, in the rare event that you have any) cautiously, to snipe at Shermans and M5s; you can usually win these encounters as long as you aren't ambushed yourself.

Usually it's not worth the effort to focus on destroying American AT guns; they can't move, so you can just pull back, rendering them ineffective by default. Pulling back, it should be noted, is a great strategy in general. Shoot, kill, and run; repeat as

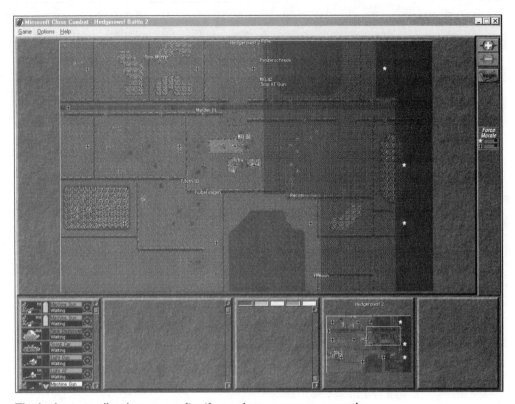

The hedgerows allow long range fire if you place your men correctly.

necessary, moving from one hedgerow to another. Don't worry, no one is going to tell the Gestapo.

Infiltration can be effective, but it is also risky. In some cases, when the American advance leaves gaps on its flanks, infiltration is a great way to shower Purple Hearts on the enemy. Most of the time, however, any teams infiltrating will get chewed up by close-in American firepower.

IT'S THE MEN THAT MATTER

The game focuses more on casualties and morale than on VP locations, and so should you. The default set ups are usually bad; they put too much of your firepower up front where the Americans will grind it into sauerkraut, or well away from the battle where it is of little use. Re-deploy your troops away from the front lines. Let the Americans

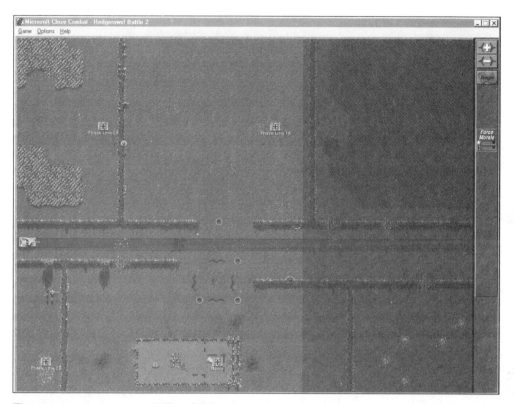

These open spots are great killing fields.

cross the first phase line, take their initial VP spots, and then massacre them when they advance across the open fields.

Don't get caught in a short range blasting match. Even in an ambush, short range fire-fights are more a matter of luck than skill. American short range firepower is powerful, and their numbers will tell. Sometimes you can defend a stone building fronted by a hedgerow; in that case, you can blast the Yanks when they crawl over the hedge, kill most of the them, and then either withdraw or hold depending on the situation. Always remember that you can't win if you die, but you can win if you run away and kill in the process.

Put your armor on roads, or in clear areas with access to roads. Usually, if your assault gun is covering a road, you'll get the first shot and often a quick kill. Armored, mobile machine guns and a cannon are a soldier's best friend sometimes, however, so be careful. You have the advantage being on the defensive, but the enemy has numbers.

Halftracks, *Kubelwagons*, and armored cars are little more than mobile machine guns. Use them with care, as they can die quickly; belly up to a hedgerow and fire away from beyond bazooka range, and withdraw if you see Shermans. Don't be afraid to shuttle your armor to hot spots; that's what the *panzertruppen* get paid for. Avoid fair fights. The American tanks react faster than your assault guns. Ambush them, use infantry AT teams and Panzerfausts when possible. Think biblical: thou shalt not suffer a tank to live.

And living is the name of the game. Pay attention to your men. The German player has the dubious advantage of having comparatively few troops. You can thus keep a closer eye on individual teams. Watch the ones that contain men of insufficient motivation (those that frequently end up with acts of cowardice indicated on the post-battle info screens). These sub-par troops should be used in the rear, while those men eager to find out where the Iron Crosses grow should be used at the sharp end. Particularly after you've decisively defeated a couple of attacks, don't hesitate to fall

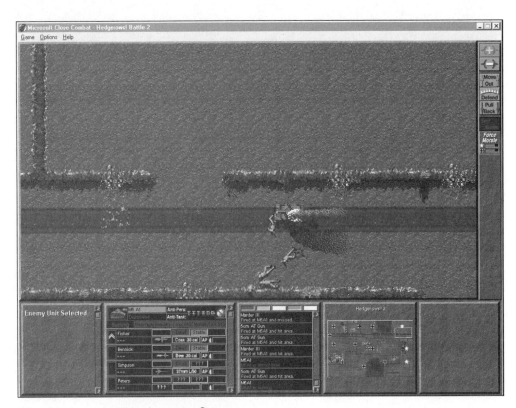

What happens when Marder meets Stuart . . .

back and play it safer. The time you've already gained will cushion the blow of any minor defeats.

. . . and what happens when more guests arrive.

8

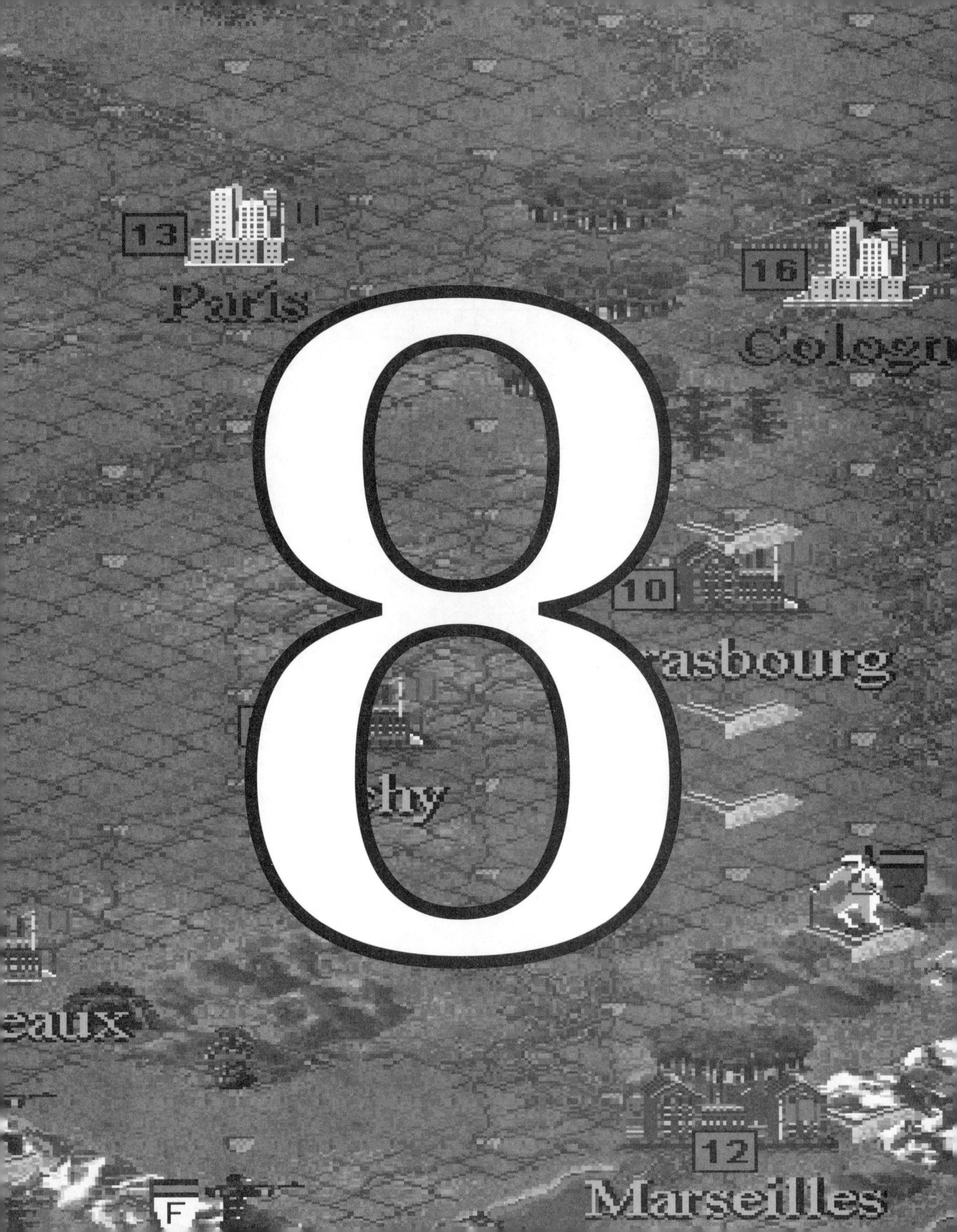

Fantasy General: A Fantasy Game Even a War Gamer Can Love

M ost hard-core war gamers would normally shun any game that has a dragon on the cover. *Fantasy General*, however, is a war game in *fantasy* clothing; there's a reason it's named *Fantasy General*, and not *Fantasy Hero* or *Fantasy Wizard*. You will need to think less like Merlin and more like Patton if you want to win *this* war!

VARIETY IS THE SPICE OF LIFE

Fantasy General presents the player with an initially bewildering plethora of choices. You can play as one of four leaders, each with his or her advantages and disadvantages, and much like the blind men and the elephant, how the game looks and plays will be greatly affected by this initial choice. Pay attention to the bonuses each leader receives, as these bonuses will determine the optimal composition of your forces. If, as Knight Marshal Calis, you looked down your nose at magical units, considering them weak and ineffective, you may find that those same units are your pride and joy when playing as Archmage Krell. Learning to defeat the enemy given the bonuses and constraints of each leader will demand that you be creative and open minded.

Which leads to the next point: a good general knows the strengths and weaknesses of his troops, and you will too if you want to have any choice of surviving through the last battle. With 180 different unit types, you will need to take the time to determine what are your troops' capabilities. As my 95-year-old grandma used

CD-ROM
Check out the CD-ROM included in this book for the demo version of *Fantasy General*.

The following image content is part of the game interface screenshot:

Campaign Game

Play A Scenario   Play In The Arena   Load Saved Game
                                                     Load PBM Turn

Background   Change Name   Army

The Knight Marshal was raised from childhood to fight evil in any form. He has devoted his life to moving among the people, helping those who strive to overcome fear and the desperation of living.

Advantages

Limited Spell Caster
Cavalry Recruiter
Charismatic
Healer

Heavy Cavalry
Cavalry
Melee: 11
Armor: 13
Movement: 5
Search Range: 3

Difficulty

Easy   Medium
Hard   Custom

Knight Marshal Calis

Start Game
Credits
Quit Game

Your choice of leader determines your optimal force composition.

to say, everybody ought to do what they do best; that's good advice when deploying troops. Study the tables in the back of the manual and determine what a unit's strengths are, and then strive constantly to keep that unit in situations that take advantage of its strength and avoids its weaknesses.

Specific tips will be covered later in this chapter, but as an example of taking advantage of strengths, Archers provide covering defensive fire for adjacent friendly units. This fire is not countered, i.e., it is a completely *free* attack and can be very deadly if used properly. However, Archers were not meant to be engaged in hand-to-hand combat, and will quickly be decimated if you allow enemy units to close and attack. Thus, the effective use of Archers is directly behind the lines of your front-line heavy hitters, creating a synergy that then results in front-line units that can attack with strength, yet are defended well enough to make the enemy pay a heavy toll when he attempts to counter-attack.

KEEP YOUR EYE ON THE PRIZE

Winning the war in *Fantasy General* requires winning your objectives, and winning your objectives requires focus. There are two types of objectives in *Fantasy General* battles: territorial and destruction of the enemy. Lose sight of your battle objectives at the risk of being presented with an annoyingly abrupt "You Lose" screen. If your objective is to destroy a percentage of the enemy units, do not allow yourself to become so distracted by capturing shrines, temples, and cities that you allow the enemy to regroup, repair, or escape.

Similarly, if your objective is to capture several locations, avoid the temptation to focus on slaughtering the enemy if doing so keeps you from taking your objectives within the allotted time. It is easy to fall into the trap of massing your forces in one section of the map, furiously mounting masterful combined arms attacks and obliterating the poor enemy, only to realize that time has run short and there are two remaining towns to capture on the other side of the mountains.

This is right where you want the enemy.

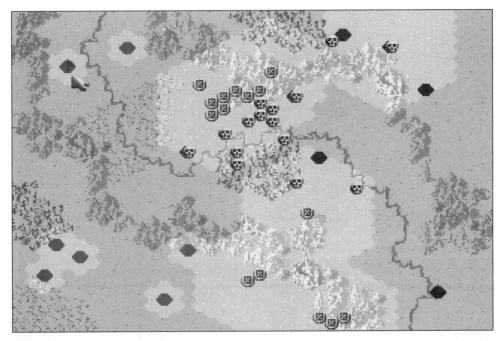

Pressing the attack, all appears safe . . .

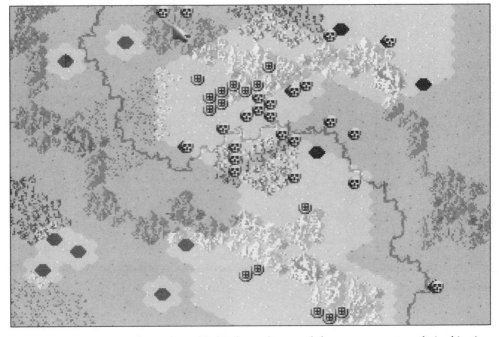

. . . but two enemy units have slipped behind your lines and threaten to capture their objective.

In the same manner, pay particular attention to the black flags representing enemy objectives. Forces driven smugly through hell and high water, cutting a swath through the apparently out-*generaled* forces of evil and within fingertip reach of capturing the last of one's objectives, can suddenly be presented with a screen informing the player of the loss of the war. Try turning off the hidden movement during such a battle and you will notice the computer sneaking a couple of units behind your lines toward his objective, completely undefended. Game over. Lesson learned. Don't leave the enemy's objective(s) unguarded. A unit or two, strategically placed, can serve as a warning picket, preventing surprise rear attacks.

In territorial objective battles, be wary of enemy units that you see once, but then disappear from sight. There's a good chance that they are trying to sneak behind your lines and obtain a cheap victory.

Force the enemy to fight in the river.

This is Light Infantry terrain.

LIFE (AND WAR) AIN'T FAIR

The last thing a good general wants is a fair fight. Your responsibility to your troops is to give them the best possible odds over their enemies. In *Fantasy General* this translates into learning how to take advantage of everything that can tip the scales a little (and sometimes a lot!) your way.

First and simplest: use the terrain to your advantage. Understand the effect that terrain has on attackers and defenders. Rivers are a great example of how you can use terrain to your benefit. A unit placed on a river hex will attack and defend at half strength. You should *never* allow your units to conduct combat while placed in a river hex. At the same time, you can often deploy your forces such that the enemy is forced to enter a river hex to get at your units. Very few sights are as pretty as watching a strong enemy unit, up to his waist in water, attempting to do battle with one of your units that is supported by archers and other support units!

Your cavalry directly north of town has no retreat path.

Similarly, while you may find Light Infantry to be of limited value, their attack bonus in heavy terrain can be an odds-tipper when forced to fight on a rugged battlefield. They can often track down and hurt Heavy Infantry units bogged down in poor terrain.

Try to avoid head-to-head battles of attrition between equally matched units. Always soften up a powerful enemy, preferably with attacks he cannot counter, such as Bombardiers, Archers, Siege Engine, Skirmishers, and spells, before directly attacking with a melee. If possible, it is preferable to have the enemy unit adjacent to at least three friendlies, as every friendly unit past the second unit gets a +4 added to their attack. Finally, try to position the enemy unit such that it is surrounded by other units, friendly and enemy. The CRT of *Fantasy General* appears to come up with a retreat result rather often, and a unit with no clear path of escape will be forced to surrender. This is an important fact to remember when positioning your own units. While it is tempting to pile up two or three unbroken lines of front-line troops, short range support, and long range support troops, doing so creates a trap for your front line troops.

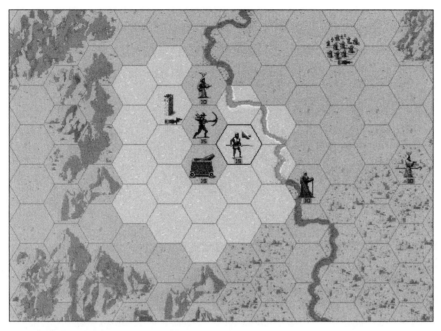

Heavy Infantry is normally stopped by the river . . .

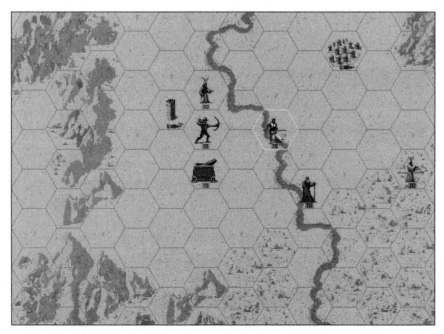

. . . but cast Forced March at the end of the normal move . . .

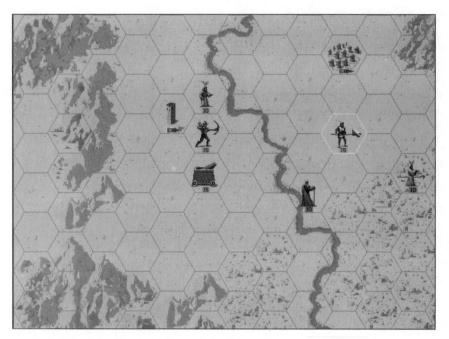

. . . and the unit easily moves beyond the river.

With moderate damage and no clear path to retreat, an otherwise very salvageable unit may be forced to surrender. Always leave some room for units to retreat as well as room to enable you to rotate your units, replacing damaged troops with fresh ones.

In the spirit of *not playing fair* and taking advantage of every edge you can get, here's a nifty trick you can use with your Heavy Infantry once they receive the Force March spell. If you cast the spell at the beginning of the unit's move, it will receive extra moves, but once the unit marches into *stopping* terrain, such as a river, your infantry will halt, regardless of remaining moves. By using the unit's normal move allotment to march into the river, and then using the Force March spell, the unit will be able to continue for a couple of moves past the normally impassable terrain.

"THEY'RE WAVING THE WHITE FLAG, SIR"

Often, when defeat is inevitable, the enemy will offer to surrender. Should you accept? The obvious benefit of accepting is the guarantee that you will win the battle and advance in your campaign. You may feel that success is inevitable and it may well be. However, should you reject the surrender, there is always the slight chance that on the

Do you accept the surrender?

last turn the enemy will, for example, retake an objective and cost you the battle. You may also want to accept a surrender if you have some units that are in danger of being eliminated.

However, there are significant benefits to rejecting a surrender. If there are towns or temples or other sites that you have not yet captured, you may decline a surrender in order to reap the gold, heroes, and other special items these sites offer. Also, by continuing the battle, you are able to give your units the added experience gained by mopping up the remaining bad guys. In general, the benefits of declining the surrender usually outweigh accepting it.

LOSE A BATTLE, LOSE THE WAR!

Fantasy General's wealth of options, including four leader personas, each with distinct advantages and disadvantages, combined with 180 unit types, result in a game with an almost unlimited variety of potential strategies. Just as air superiority can determine the outcome of a war in real life, so can control of the sky determine the outcome of a *Fantasy General* battle. The wise general will purchase Sky Hunters and Bombardiers early in the campaign, giving them time to gain experience and upgrade. As with all unit types in the game, their effectiveness will be directly proportional to your ability to take advantage of their strengths and avoid their weaknesses.

Sky Hunters are your fighter/attack air units. Their primary uses will include killing enemy Sky Hunters, protecting your units most vulnerable to enemy Sky Hunters (such as Bombardiers, Siege weapons, and Archers), and attacking the enemy's support units that cannot be safely attacked by your ground units. Their great mobility also makes them excellent for chasing down and finishing off any crippled enemy ground forces

This Bombardier needs fighter support!

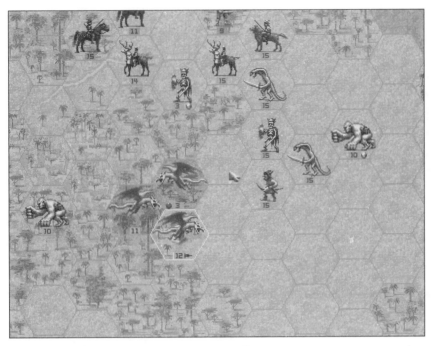

Use pairs of Sky Hunters to finish off enemy flyers.

that attempt to retreat to safety. That same high degree of mobility allows Sky Hunters themselves to quickly retreat long distances when damaged; take advantage of this capability to allow your crippled Sky Hunters to recuperate, and make sure that you track down and finish off the enemy's damaged flyers.

When retreating your own hurt flyers, it is safest to have them hover over a ground unit, such as Archers, that can provide protection against enemy air attack. High mobility plus an inability to be attacked by most ground forces also allows these units to excel as scouts. Quality is much more important than quantity with these units; as the manual correctly points out, two high-level Sky Hunters are much more valuable than four entry-level Sky Hunters. High-level flyers, such as the Phoenix Hawks, with their 22 magical melee attack, Raise Dead spell, and invulnerability to magic, are truly awesome weapons.

Bombardiers are very analogous to the traditional bomber aircraft of WWII. They are best used to soften up tough enemy ground units, such as experienced Heavy Infantry, before you throw your own ground units against them. Like traditional real world bombers, they are very vulnerable to fighter aircraft (Sky Hunters) and, if the

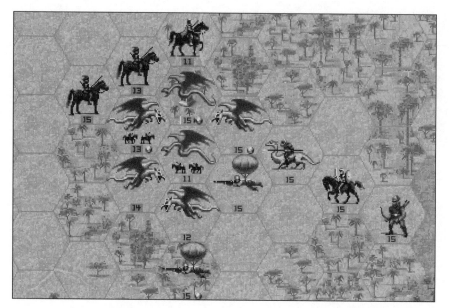

Outnumbered in the air!

enemy has a strong air force, require strong friendly air support to survive. They are also vulnerable to attack by Archers and Siege Weapons.

Consider this creative use of magic: equip a Bombardier with a magical Staff that is effective against flyers, such as the Staff of Winds or Storm Staff. You now have a fighter/bomber that can provide a nasty little surprise when attacked by an unsuspecting Sky Hunter!

SPEED KILLS (THE ENEMY, THAT IS)

Chess players know the importance of time in developing an attack; the German army taught the world the effectiveness of the *blitzkrieg* in WWII. *Fantasy General* provides ample motivation for the wise general to move swiftly. First and most obviously, each battle has a time limit in which to accomplish your objectives.

There are other reasons to strike quickly, however. The computer AI is given a fairly significant level of reinforcement late in each battle. By quickly reaching enemy towns, cities, and castles, you can prevent the enemy from building and recruiting additional units. Even if you haven't yet captured the site, having a ground unit adjacent to the site prevents the enemy from obtaining additional forces from there. (Note

A pair of Siege Engines provide powerful anti-aircraft support.

that only adjacent ground units prevent building and recruiting—flying forces have no such effect.)

Also, by moving rapidly you can make the enemy adapt to your plans rather than vice versa. For example, effective use of rivers gives your forces an advantage; the difference between which side has to fight out of the river is often a matter of who can first set up their forces in the optimal position. Lastly, time is critical in finding certain heroes; if you are late, the hero is unavailable to join your forces.

So, how does one gain the edge in speed? First, look at the map and develop your plan before the battle begins. You cannot afford to just move your units and see what

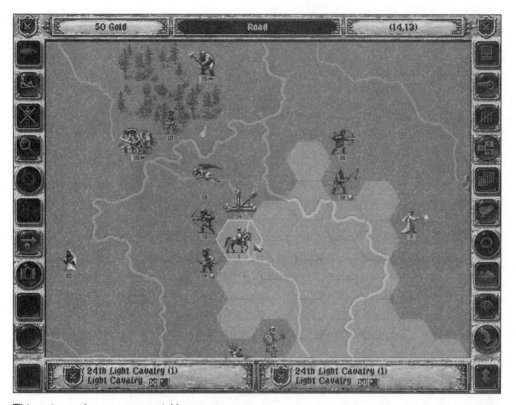

This unit needs to retreat, quickly.

the enemy has in store for you; you must be proactive, not reactive. Use your faster troops to establish the positions you wish to fight from, as well as scout out where the opposition is located. If you are racing the enemy to a favored fighting position, such as adjacent to a river, use your more mobile units (e.g., Cavalry and flyers) to harass and tie up and thus slow down the enemy troops. Beware, however, of outrunning your support units (Archers, Siege Engines) and being forced to attack and defend without their assistance.

The relatively slow speed of Archers and particularly Siege weapons is a problem that is best minimized by paying attention to the order in which you move your forces (to avoid blocking the roads). Also, healing spells can be great boons to keeping your forces moving forward. Healing a damaged unit with a spell can save three turns worth of movement: the retreating move to safety, the stationary turn to rest and heal, and then the next move that returns the unit back to its original position. Three turns can be enough to turn the course of a battle!

NOTHING UP MY SLEEVE . . .

Be creative with the use of magic. Combining spells and magic items with various unit types can create forces with interesting capabilities. Recall the previous mention of giving a Staff with capability to attack flyers to a Bombardier to create a fighter/bomber. Giving a Staff of Healing to a flyer creates a highly mobile hospital—a flying M.A.S.H. unit!

If you have a unit with an Animate Trees spell, it can be highly effective to force enemy forces to either retreat into woods, or even better, lure them into the woods; then cast the spell and let the trees do your dirty work! (Shades of the Wizard of OZ!) A Magic Javelin given to an infantry unit allows it to counterattack those pesky Skirmishers. Placing a Death Wound spell on an experienced, high-level Heavy Infantry or Heavy Cavalry unit results in all Wounds inflicted by that unit transforming to Deaths; such units can be monsters on the battlefield!

The Death Wound spell can turn the tide of battle.

Speaking of magic, don't forget that the Magic Resistance value for a unit is taken into account not only for spells, but for direct magic attacks (melee or skirmish). The tables in the manual show which units have magical vs. physical attacks. The armor value on a seemingly impregnable unit may be largely negated if it takes a magic attack and its magic resistance is low. Use this to your advantage; giving a unit a magical weapon suddenly gives it a boost in damage inflicted and a reduction in the mortal enemy's armor rating.

Spellcasters are an interesting breed. While some have reported success with armies predominated by magic units, their weakness in direct, melee attacks dictates the need to protect them with stronger mortal forces. Magic units can increase in experience, but remember that they can never be upgraded. My experience is that spellcasters can be very effective support units, attacking enemy support forces such as Archers, but you must ensure they are kept away from enemy melee units.

This Spellcaster is too close to the action.

MECH MY DAY

If you rescue Ferras the Mechmaster during the campaign, you will receive the ability to purchase Mech units. You must also rescue Niels the Engineer to be able to repair them. Mech units are a mixed blessing. It is nice to have access to an entirely new set of interesting units, but be aware that your research on other unit types is now split with the Mechs, slowing down the progress of new Magic or Mortal forces. Mech armor ratings are quite high and their attack values tend to be relatively high, particularly against the significant number of enemy units that are specifically vulnerable to Mechs. On the down side, Mechs are very vulnerable to magic attacks, and as the campaign progresses you will face an increasingly large number of enemy magical units, turning your Mechs into liabilities.

This chapter presents a very small sampling of strategy hints and tips that are applicable to Fantasy General. The pleasure of this game is the almost infinite approaches that can be devised and tested; this is a no-one-path-to-victory program. Experiment and enjoy!

Knight Marshal Calis is the victor!

The result of a well-executed strategy is shown here.

9

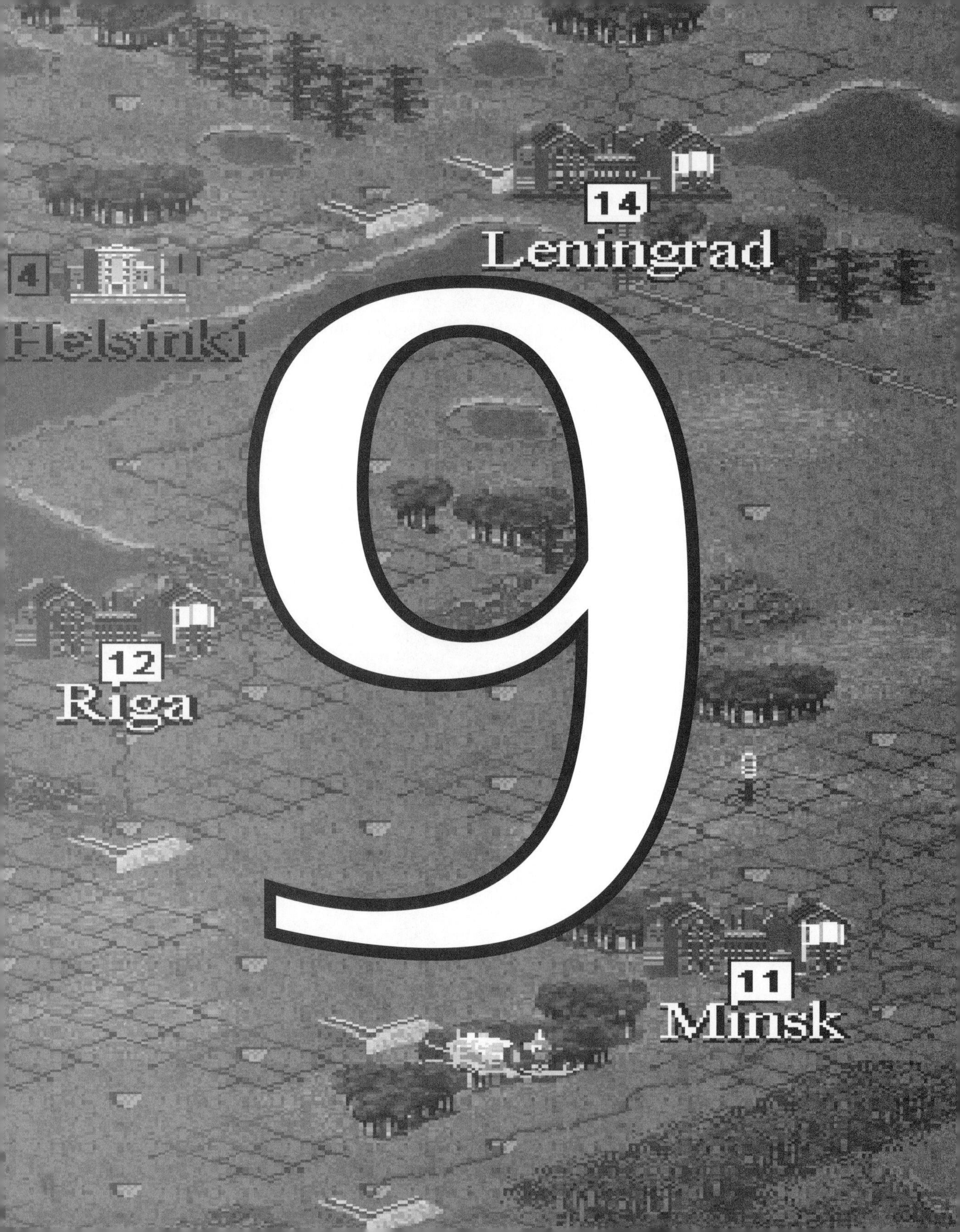

Allied General

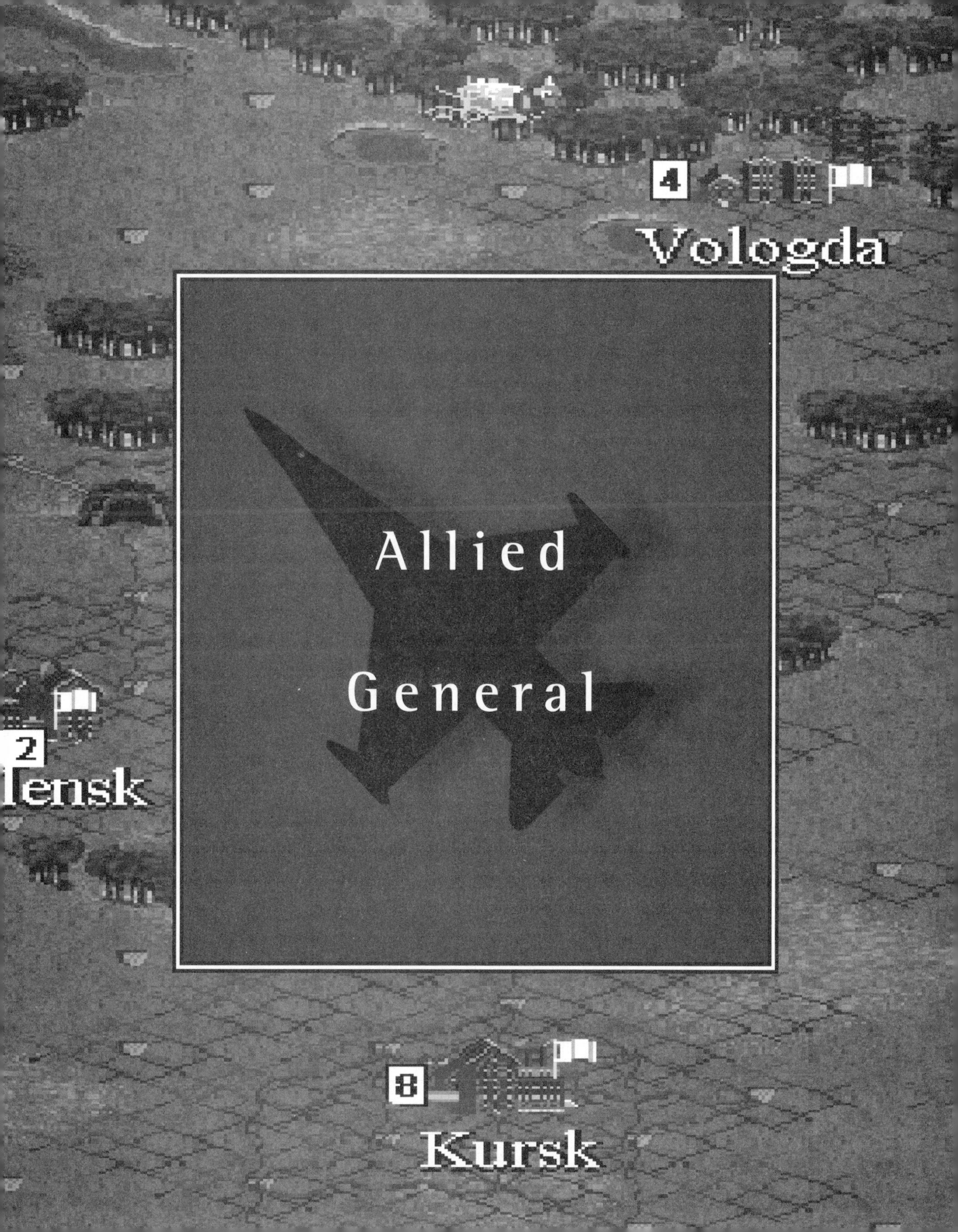

Behold the tips and secrets that will help you grab your own piece of real estate! Send in troops to capture you a bit of North Africa, Europe, or Russia. The time will come when a piece of real estate must be held.

SOLVING THE PUZZLE

Determining strategy hints and tips for *Allied General* is a lot like researching RPG hints and tips and less like unlocking the secrets of warfare. Oh sure, it matters where, when, and how each of the units are employed. However, more important is the gamer's ability to solve the puzzle inherent to the game system in general and each scenario in particular. To that end, rather than plop a multipage treatise on unit employment in your lap, this chapter will attempt to help you solve some of *Allied General*'s puzzles.

TAKE THE INITIATIVE

Perhaps the key to winning *Allied General* battles is initiative. Frequently this is overlooked, and understandably so, because in the *Allied General* rule book the discussion of initiative consists of a whopping four lines. To understand the importance of initiative let's first review the *Allied General* combat engine.

A lot happens when the gamer places the crosshairs and clicks. *Allied General* utilizes an interval versus odds based combat results table (CRT). In other words, eleven attack factors versus five defense factors is resolved on the +6, versus 2:1, column of the computer's notional CRT. Each combatant attacks once per unsuppressed strength point

it possesses. Kills are permanent; suppression, with the exception of that inflicted by level bombers, only effects the current combat.

In this type of resolution system who attacks first is pivotal. *Allied General* determines this by comparing the participants' initiative rating and adding a random number between zero and two. The contestant with the higher final initiative shoots first. This allows a unit with strong initiative to minimize damage to itself by killing or suppressing enemy strength points before they have attacked.

There are several ways of using this to your advantage. Entrenchment, experience, and terrain modifications are reflected in initiative versus attack or defense bonuses. Obviously, gamers should maximize terrain benefits. Remember, a unit that doesn't move will assume the baseline entrenchment value of its terrain. For example, units in a city will get a +4 entrenchment modifier—a powerful edge when added to baseline initiative. Because experience is another modifier it is useful to keep your experienced units alive. Pull them out of the line early, before the enemy can mount multiple killing assaults on them. Like the manual says, to avoid watering down veteran units' experience, only give them elite replacements. Anti-tank guns, although blessed with high initiative, *always* fire last when attacking. And look before you leap; when a unit stumbles into an ambush—which triggers a rugged defense—its initiative is set to zero.

Interestingly, the real world effects of first fire have been well documented. In a study conducted subsequent to WW II it was determined that an attacking force outnumbered 2:1 that fired first had a higher chance of success than one with a 5:1 superiority that fired second. For sure, much of current military technological research (i.e., sighting and gun ballistics) is aimed at increasing our forces' chance to be the first to engage. Just remember, what you kill first can't shoot back at you.

CRACKING NUTS

Nevertheless, a gamer armed with the truths we've just revealed will still find *Allied General* to be a tough nut to crack. If you have grown impatient of beating your head against a wall of panzers the following *solutions* are offered for the British campaign in North Africa.

Sidi Barrani is a nice warm up. It's nearly impossible *not* to win this encounter. What is important is how big you win. As is the case with most *Allied General* face-offs the degree of victory is not only determined by how many objectives are captured but how quickly. In this case, the points of contention are Tobruk and Benghazi.

Tobruk is a straightforward demonstration of combined arms warfare, *Allied General* style. The key to the city's capture is the Italian 75mm artillery. British infantry

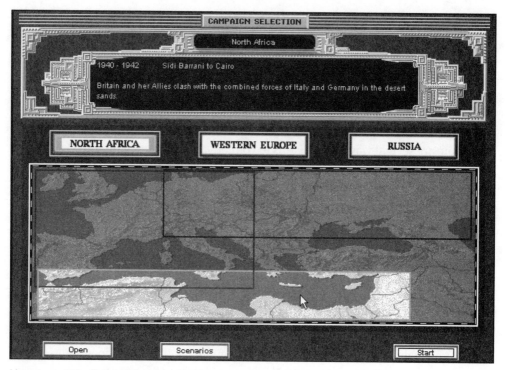

Here is a view of the campaign window.

assaults prior to this unit's neutralization are sure to suffer some serious casualties from defensive artillery. In the initiative equation discussed above, defensive artillery fires before all else, reducing that beautiful British infantry to a paltry two or three effective strength points. So first pound the Italian artillery formation with the 25 pounders, then follow with an infantry assault on the 47mm AT unit. Two of the Tommies' formations should be enough to make these Italians seek the better part of valor. Now you are ready to attack Tobruk with the final two infantry units. The Matilda IIs can exploit for the capture. The speed of Tobruk's fall is critical. The British can bludgeon past the Italians regardless of the tactics employed. However, using a scalpel is quicker—and costs fewer prestige points for replacements.

After Tobruk is taken, the British must resist the urge to shove their entire army down the coastal road. Due to a couple of well-placed Italian blocking positions, road-bound units may not arrive in time to capture Benghazi. Most of the victors from the battle of Tobruk (especially the truck-mounted units) must take this route. However, at least one tank unit (preferably the A13 with its relatively high soft attack factor)

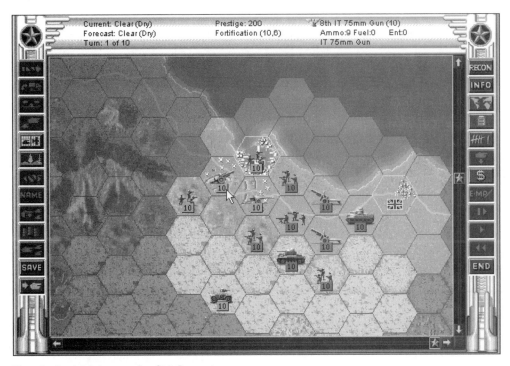

Here is the initial setup for Sidi Barrani.

accompanied by a Bren Carrier mounted infantry should plow through the desert to assail Benghazi from the south. Hopefully, this two-pronged assault will crush the Italian defenses and earn a major victory.

With a major (victory that is) in your pocket it's time to move on to El Agheila. This is tougher fare. The British must first absorb the Nazis' onslaught before they can attempt to capture El Agheila; at least that's how it seems. However, using this absorb-then-thrust philosophy often garners no better than a handful of minor victories. Although you can turn the Germans away from Tobruk, your armor may be unable to wade through the endless hordes of PZ I/IIs the Germans built to defend the Mechili-Mersa Brega pass. Obviously, the bad guys were getting way too many prestige points. As in Sidi Barrani, the secret lay to the south.

The almost road-like path of clear terrain from Bardia/Sidi Barrani to El Agheila is the clue. Send a Matilda II, HW infantry, and an A9 through it. Use the Mosquito as this task force's flying artillery. Capture whichever is easier, Mersa Brega or El Agheila and build, build, build.

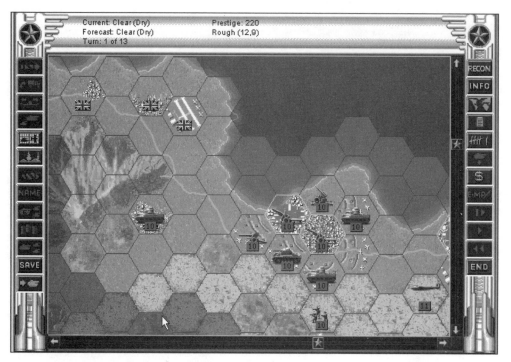

Here's the initial setup for El Agheila.

Meanwhile, back at the northern ranch, the Nazis will be pressing hard across the front. The initial deployment builds and placement will go far in determining if the Empire can hold the line. Bolster Benghazi's defenses with a 3" air defense unit and a Matilda II. Cyrene guard duties were given to a '39 infantry who, once play begins, will advance south through the Benghazi-Mechili mountains to blunt any German moves through this tough terrain. This left a 2 pounder, HW infantry, 3" air defense, and Matilda II, supported by artillery to defend Tobruk against the wave of German metal. No, it's not easy. But if the Queen's men can hold 'til Mersa Brega and El Agheila are captured, Rommel's lack of prestige coupled with the pressure of the British in his rear should collapse the Afrika Korps.

If El Agheila is hard, Mersa El Brega is insane. Without a large (let's say 750) prestige point stash from El Agheila the British are going nowhere fast. The Germans have too many high-quality units and a seemingly endless supply of prestige points to back them up.

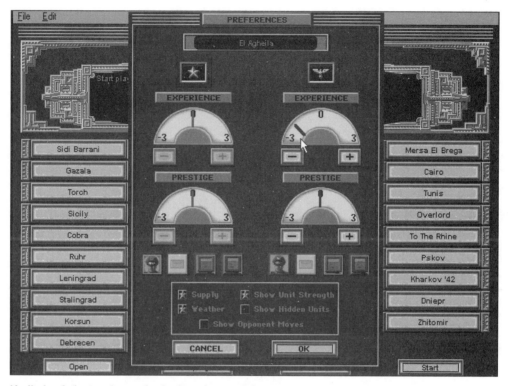

If all else fails, just lower the bad guy's morale!

During the initial deployment the British are given the option of upgrading their armor to those snazzy looking Grants, but think twice before doing so. Although faster and better able to blast infantry (that 75mm really does a job on them) they are unable to take punishment like the Matildas. Upgrade one and use it to escort speedy Bren mounted infantry but keep a couple of Matildas for the tough work.

Here's the game plan: Defend Benghazi with two infantry, a 3" air defense unit and a Matilda II. These should advance to Bir El Gobi and hold on for dear life. Place an anti-tank gun and another 3" plane killer in Bir Bevid. With luck they will hold, without it they will at least slow the Wehrmacht. Send a task force of whatever can be patched together west along the southern board edge. Their goal is to capture El Agheila (didn't you do this before?).

The point of this aggressive defense is prestige point denial. The Wehrmacht will soon overwhelm a passive British defense. However, if the Tommies can strangle the bad guys' prestige, the Afrika Korps' attack will fade to black. The southern thrust

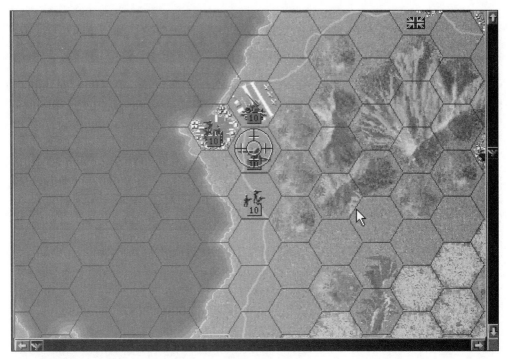

Enemy infantry are an ATG's worst enemy.

serves the dual purpose of not only capturing vital hexes but forcing the German to peel units from their northern attack. Perhaps Rommel's minions will falter early enough to allow the British to recapture their lost territory. If not, the Axis will win.

Certainly these *solutions* are not the only road to victory. In some cases, they may not even be the best. Nevertheless, if we gave away all the secrets, it would take all the fun out of playing. Besides, there is also the issue of strategic defense, so let's take a look at that now.

DEFENSE IN THE LESS GLAMOROUS WAR

A great deal has been written on taking the offense in *Allied General*. From the game's README file, which includes a rather extensive treatise on the blow-by-blow capture

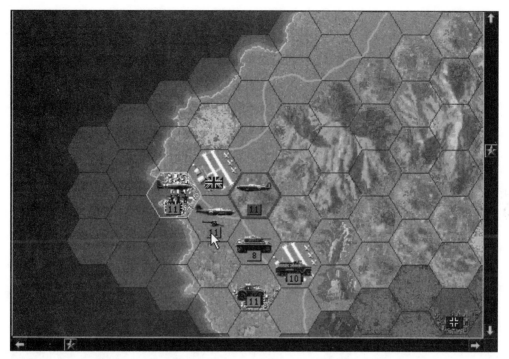

Air superiority is crucial in *Allied General*.

of objectives, to the pages of the World Wide Web, which are awash with cyber surfers discussing the best way to seize Tobruk, Berlin, or St.-Lô, much ink has been spilled on the subject. No doubt, attacking is the meat of the game. Nevertheless, obtaining the overwhelming force necessary to capture one portion of the battlefield will frequently require holding in another. To this end, covering some basic tenets on *Allied General* defense might prove helpful to the silicon-based Pattons and Montgomerys of the world.

THE BEST DEFENSE . . .

Okay, so you've heard it a thousand times, from football to laying blame on co-workers—the best defense is a good offense. Don't sit there and take what your opponent is shoving down your throat, stand up and lay into him. *Allied General* is no exception. Seizing the initiative directs the action where you want it—away from your opponent's objectives. This works best against humans as the computer's artificial intelligence may not respond to your attempts to refocus the flow of the battle.

On the other hand, the CPU's refusal (or rather inability) to react may work to your advantage. In many *Allied General* scenarios the Nazis seem to have an insurmountable number of units (Hey, nobody claimed this was an historical war game). Killing them all may be more than a little difficult. Why not take them out before they are born? That's right, constantly be on the lookout for ways of denying prestige points to the motherboard. Flank attacks by small task forces, paradrops, and amphibious assaults are all methods to pull a surprise coup on a lightly defended city. If you have air superiority, bomb the hell out of the bad guy's cities with level bombers.

LEAN ON ME

Despite the previously mentioned offensive minded ploys, the time will come when a piece of real estate must be held, pure and simple. There are two critical elements to the holding: proper utilization of supporting units and terrain.

The three types of supporting units in *Allied General* are artillery, the air defense family, and fighters. Each has a key role in defending. Due to their ability to provide

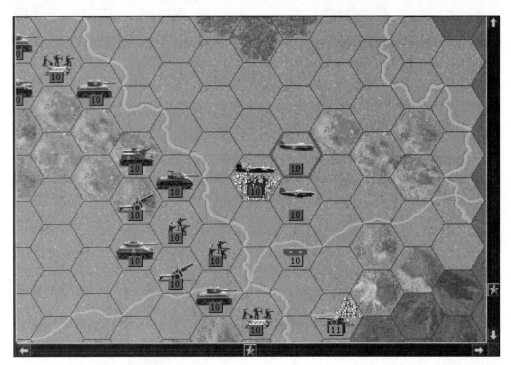

Bombing 'em into submission.

defensive fire to adjacent units artillery is a must for any successful defense. Remember, the pivotal aspect of the *Five Star Series* is initiative. Artillery provides defensive fire before the initiative is calculated for the attack proper, and suppressed enemy strength points stay that way for the ensuing attack. Obviously, the artillery should be placed to provide support to the most units without allowing a direct attack on itself.

Air defense units provide a function similar to artillery. In this case however, protection is provided to adjacent units from air attack. Place these guys to primarily protect the artillery. The easiest way for the bad guys to dismantle a defense is by first taking out the artillery with air attacks. The air defense units may get them to think twice.

Ditto for aircraft, especially fighters. In order to bomb a unit the bomber must be in the hex. If your fighter is already there it will first have to be eliminated. This adds another layer on the onion the attacker must peel in order to capture his objective.

Terrain is a strange bird in *Allied General*. Certainly, geography works in a manner familiar to war gamers—units in the city, mountains, etc, are tough; those in the clear are not. Yet the software's method is a tad curious. Rather than add a bonus to

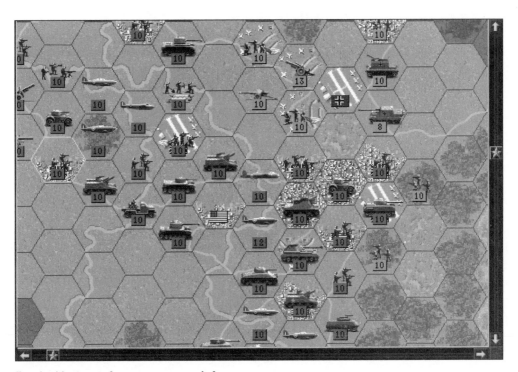

For the Nazis too few men, too much front.

a unit's defense factor, terrain places a cap on the attacking unit's initiative—frequently enabling the defender to fire first. For example, the clear terrain cap is 99 (unlimited) while the cap for units defending in a forest or city is three and one, respectively. That will cut those Panthers' initiative down to size!

While certainly not the most glamorous part of *Allied General*, sound defensive tactics are critical to the gamer's ability to win, especially in the campaign game, where defending one location with the minimum number of units is necessary to conduct an offense on the other side of the screen with overwhelming force. Hopefully, the above will assist in your endeavors to smash the wicked Boche within your computer, log on to the Internet, and splash some ink on a new subject.

10

1

n Sierra's Cyberstorm you take control in the ultimate battle for the future of

humankind by commanding destructive warriors in the form of genetically engineered

Bioderms. By linking the Bioderms to Herc pilots, you create a fighting force capable

of carrying out multiple missions to bring down the deadly Cybrids.

CYBRID INCURSION: THE GEHENNA CAMPAIGN

Throughout campaigns over multiple worlds you can plan and execute, upgrade weapons, and even manipulate genetic structures. Here we'll cover a raid of the deadly Cybrids in the Gehenna Campaign.

DELTA-2A/1: HERC MANAGEMENT

Remember that each Herc chassis supports different combinations of weapons. For example, the Shadow can carry lasers and missiles but can't support cannon and other ballistic weapons. If you're on a planet with unpredictable atmospherics that stuff up your beams and homers, this crate isn't for you.

The other effect of a unique chassis is that each has its own vulnerabilities. Some Hercs can carry long-range weapons but minimal close-in protection. Force Leader Zack found this out the hard way when his pair of Demons got fried by a swarm of Parasites porting ELF beams; they raced into close range before he

CD-ROM
Check out the CD-ROM included in this book for the demo version of *Cyberstorm*.

could track 'em, and escaped with nary a scratch. Always purchase Hercs in mutually supporting pairs; the buddy system allows your 'derms to protect each others' flanks, as well as pick on single cybrids that come too close.

Choose Hercs and systems appropriate to the mission you've chosen. If the planet has low G, send your ballistic shots into orbit and then ditch your cannons and take something else. You get full credit on all sales, so feel free to scrap your Herc fleet at any stage and rebuild from scratch.

Selling and purchasing Hercs continually can take literally hours in the Herc Bay, tinkering with weapon configs and system setups; save yourself the time by saving a few *stock* Hercs using the Save Herc Configuration option. This will allow you to rebuild a complete fleet in minutes, with only minor adjustments required before battle. Having identical weapons configs for each Herc class also makes tactical decisions on the battlefield easier.

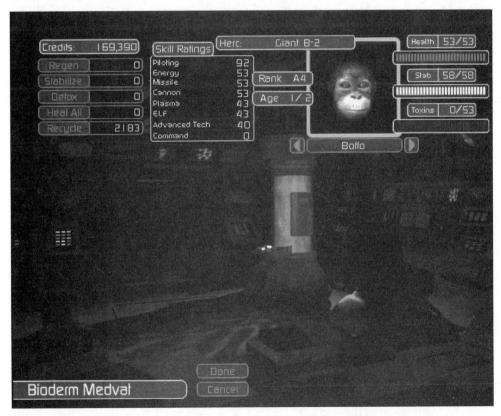

Meet Boffo the wonder chimp, complete with attitude problem and loose diapers—the only 'derm whose Herc ports a pooper-scooper.

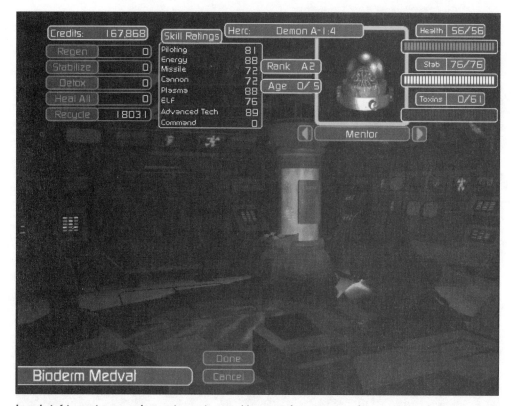

In a brief jump into an alternative universe, Mentor takes time out from training Lensmen and lazily enjoys his nutrient bath.

Don't leave your credits at base; you don't gain any interest, and the other recruits will try to nick 'em while you're out in the field. If you think your current mission could be bloody and you're saving your dimes for future repairs, you're probably performing the wrong mission; pick an easier one and spend all your creds on Hercs and 'derms.

Upgrade your Hercs at every opportunity, because the Cybrids surely will. When you get a promotion, you also gain new technology; so don't be afraid to use it.

There are two types of Hercs you should be purchasing: Marauders (for doing the grunt work) and Scouts (for spotting potential targets). Configure the former with lots of powerful weapons and good shielding; don't worry about speed too much, as you'll be letting the cybrids come to you. Your scouts should be as light as possible and carry the best sensors you can buy; use them to locate cybrid concentrations, and remember to keep them out of the battle when the fireworks start. Remember that each scout is effectively one less Herc when it comes to beating up cybrids.

DELTA-2A/1-1: WEAPONS

Okay, you've arrived at the fun bit. Let's talk about serious hardware.

First rule of arming Hercs: make sure you're packing enough anti-shield systems. Most of the weapons you'll be using in the Paracelsus system require you to down cybrid shields before you can start peeling away the armor. Balance your anti-shield and anti-armor systems accordingly. Also, divide the weapons evenly across each element of your Herc pairs; this'll reduce the chances of losing all your anti-armor bite when one of your Hercs bites the dust.

Some rookies used to think that using ELF systems to dissect cybrids with active shields was a neat thing to do. Here's some free advice: leave the ELF in the woods where it belongs. The only way you're going to get the chance to use it is if you're face to face with the enemy; unless you kill 'em all during that turn, you're going to get some feral cybrid running around behind you and giving your ass a blast you'll never forget!

Take a good mix of energy and projectile weapons; once you've downed the cybrid shields with your energy weapons you'll still have the capability of damaging their internal systems with your cannons and missiles, even if you're at low power.

DELTA-2A/1-2: OTHER SYSTEMS

Use anti-grav and over-drive systems to counteract the heavy weapons and chassis you'll be using later in the campaign; a scout with both of these systems will literally fly across the surface of low-G moons and planetoids.

Don't mount mining equipment on every Herc; just configure several to do the shovel work once the enemy has been neutralized.

Always mount ECM; there's nothing more pleasing than watching four or five particle beams whizzing over your right shoulder . . . and nothing more irritating then seeing them hit!

While self-repair won't be an issue during most missions, don't neglect your nanotech systems during the final battle of each system—you'll need them then.

RHO-4Q/1: BIODERM MANAGEMENT

Always generate 'derms with long life spans. Heck, if you're forking out good creds for your troops, you want value for money; you don't want 'em 'plasing into goo when they're just getting good at their game.

Use the Virtual Reality Trainer extensively; it's cheap, effective, and greatly improves your 'derms' value in battle. Don't rely purely on expensive targeting computers; all they do is counter enemy ECM systems.

As much as you might like to assign 'derms to their rigs, Unitech does provide an effective Autolink system. As you're fighting through the Ionis cluster you may find you are relying on the linker to perform all your unit assignments. Some borderline cases do occur on occasion, so feel free to step in and adjust the pilots if you have the time.

OMEGA-9Y: BATTLEFIELD TACTICS

Here are some simple tips that'll save your butt in the field.

Concentrate your Hercs. Keeping your forces together allows you to project maximum firepower where you need it.

Maneuvering in line-abreast has several advantages. During the final battle on Beran, a solid line kept most of the enemy Verminus out of ELF (and self-destruct) range. It also provided my units with clear lines of fire; even friendly Hercs can mask your own unit's weapons. Finally, shields can be maximized to the two hexes in front of your Hercs, allowing adjacent units to shield your flanks. Only split up into small groups when you're facing a small cybrid presence and always travel in pairs.

Gang up on cybrids. Two Hercs firing at the same side of any cybrid will toast him pronto. Remember that if you shoot at cybrids from behind, they will eventually turn around and shoot back at you. It can be very frustrating having downed the shields on your target, only to see it turn and conceal its vulnerable side once more, so mass fire on individual cybrids.

When you move across the battlefield, always move short distances and make sure your available reactor and battery power is high; you'll need the energy to take reaction shots at nearby cybrids.

Enemy cybrids aren't as bright as they could be. They tend to like depressions to hide in, working on the principle that they can't be shot at. They also regard the closest Herc as the greatest threat. Use these facts in your battlefield strategy. You can use your scouts to lure the cybrids into an ambush, keeping them in small hollows or behind masking terrain at the end of each turn. Maneuver the enemy into a depression, while keeping your main force just beyond weapons range, and lure them along it until they're spread out. Finally, move your main force forward and hit them in the flank.

Always use terrain to your advantage. Right click on hexes to see what kind of offensive and defensive benefits you'll gain; that towering Zaquath tree may provide enough protection from stray rounds.

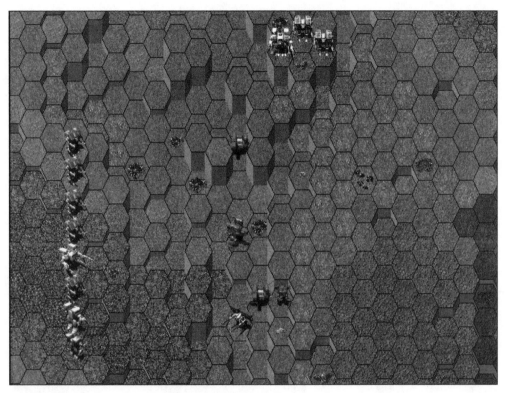

Cybrids may be thick on the ground, but the same goes for their AI. Lure them into a ravine with a small team (the guys to the north).

When you meet your victory conditions and are prompted to return to the carrier for extraction, don't do so immediately. If your Hercs are still damaged, use any remaining nanotech modules while you're still in the field; the Unitech accountants will happily recharge them for free when you return to base. Similarly, there's absolutely no reason to return to base with toxic 'derms that are as stable as jello; use those expensive life support systems to rejuvenate your crews before ending the mission. Are you on a mining mission? Well, Unitech taxes auto-mining pretty heavily, so, if you're eager to save anywhere between 2000 and 6000 credits each mission, mine the excess ore before you leave the planet. Yeah, sure it's boring, but just think how many extra Neutron guns you'll be able to buy.

2

Scapa Flow

Conquest
of the
New World

20
London

7

Amsterd

1nterplay's latest strategy title, *Conquest of the New World* (CNW), has all the hallmarks of a classic. Its blend of simple mechanics, random setups, and strong AI guarantee a riveting experience for all gamers interested in 4X type games (eXplore, eXpand, eXploit, and eXterminate.) To give you budding *conquistadors* a fighting chance in your initial games, we'll take a look at designing a *CNW* character, guidelines on getting your colonies started, and a quick and dirty guide to resolving tactical battles.

DESIGNING YOUR CHARACTER

Choosing which special abilities are appropriate for each game is dependent on a wide variety of factors. The game duration, map size, number of opponents, and what abilities they decide to choose all make picking the perfect character nigh impossible. Ultimately, the best character you can design is the one you'll be most happy playing. Don't try to second guess what your opponents are going to do. Just choose your character and try to analyze your opponents as the game progresses. If an opponent fields large armies regularly, and you know he only has a couple of forts in a single colony, you can guess he probably chose the Conqueror option. If he avoids contact with you despite having a large colony just down the road, well, he's probably a Colonist. With a bit of luck you should be able to block your opponent's ultimate goals while utilizing your own abilities to their utmost.

CD-ROM
Check out the CD-ROM included in this book for the demo version of *Conquest of the New World*.

ESTABLISHING YOUR COLONIES

When placing your first colony, try to locate an optimal site. Your initial colony is going to be the sole source of income for the first few decades, so it's vital to place it wisely. Make sure it's situated so that good terrain for generating wood and metals is available nearby. You'll also need a nearby coastline to provide you with trade capability with your home country. Always explore around a potential colony site before establishing it; you need to examine the surroundings for flat ground to ensure that when you upgrade your colony center in the future, there's plenty of room to expand into. The following table shows the best terrain for each production type.

TERRAIN PREFERENCES BY PRODUCTION IN ORDER OF PREFERENCE		
PRODUCTION/BUILDING/CROPS/FARMS	METALS/METAL MINES	GOLD/GOLD MINES
Grassland	Mountains	Mountains
Rivers (Adjacent)	Rivers (Adjacent)	Rivers (Adjacent)
Lakes/Deltas (Adjacent)	Lakes/Deltas (Adjacent)	Lakes/Deltas (Adjacent)
Oceans		
Wood/Mills		
Jungle		
Forest		
Rivers (Adjacent)		

Once you've placed your colony center, you're ready to place your initial buildings. Build as many metal mines and mills as you can (remembering to examine building sites for any terrain-based production bonuses). You'll also need a house and a farm to keep your colonists warm and healthy, and a dock to allow you to trade with your home country. Don't bother building a gold mine yet; they don't usually provide much benefit, and when you trade your stocks of metal and wood you'll rapidly build up your bank balance. Once your bank balance is looking a bit healthier, obtain some goods from home and use them to build up commercial structures. By now you should have a good colony base, providing you with lumber and wood in large quantities and a small but regular goods intake from commerce.

You'll probably notice that the large number of buildings doesn't leave much room for expansion; it's now time to upgrade your colony center. Once it's upgraded you

The colony of Cardiff faces an uncertain fate at the hands of several Dutch armies in the field; let's hope the town militia are on their toes!

can commence upgrading your initial mines and mills; this allows you to build some of the larger buildings on the newly available land.

Don't encourage your colonists to sit around idle all day. Make sure you have enough jobs to keep them occupied. Whether they work or not, they still eat just as many crops as the workers do. If your colonists start immigrating (or breeding) too quickly, act like a blasphemer and torch the churches and a house or two. Once the word gets around that you don't hold Sunday services any more, most of the lay-abouts will pack up and sail home.

By now, several new threats may have made themselves apparent. Perhaps a nearby Indian village isn't as peaceful as you'd like, or maybe the Spanish frigate loitering off the coast has you changing into spare pantaloons every time it sails by? That's right: it's time to build a fort to let them know you mean business.

When you recruit military units, make sure you generate a good mix of infantry, cavalry, and artillery, as the combat system rewards *combined arms* tactics. Make sure you keep a large force in the colony itself; Indian war parties don't announce themselves in advance, and you don't want the town militia to have to deal with them on their own. Once you have a strong garrison, you're in a position to change into a more

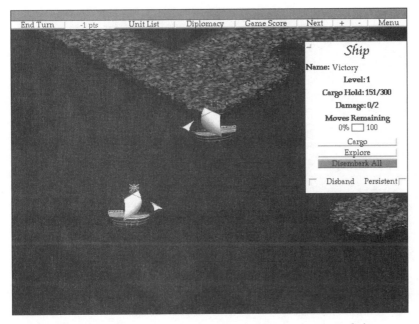

General Beaufort has found an Iroquois village; the natives must fight to the bitter end.

aggressive posture. Leaders are vital for successful military operations; now that you've upgraded your colony center, you can recruit more experienced commanders. Leaders and units improve in two ways—through better tactics gained by investing in war colleges and by gaining experience on the battlefield. A good way to gain battle experience is to attack nearby native villages. Round up a big enough force and trounce the locals with your *sticks that go boom*! Interested in how to use the tactical combat module to the utmost? Well, read on.

RESOLVING TACTICAL BATTLES

Combat on the battlefield can provide you with a brief respite from all those colony management decisions you've been making, but be warned, the computer AI is very good. I suggest you limit use of the auto combat option; sure it's quicker, but I received some very surprising defeats on a couple of key battles when I was convinced I'd win.

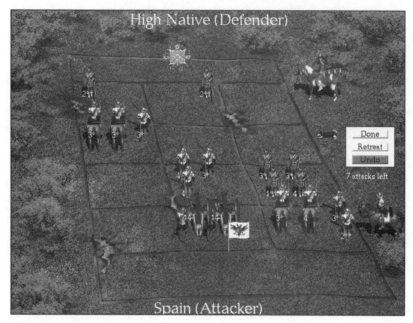

Mr. Hawkins curses the day he picked up that travel guide at the Huron village.

As the rules suggest, the two key things to look for in combat are: 1) attack a target square with as many different unit types as possible, and 2) attack from as many different squares as possible. I prefer not to advance up the center column too much; as a defender you can potentially be attacked from three sides. I usually manage to obtain a victory by placing a blocking force in the center column (with reserves available) and attacking up one (or both) flanks, provided the numerical odds are even or better.

Advancing up the flanks gives you two options: you can either threaten his center or continue towards the back row. Once you're at the back row, his artillery will be vulnerable and a crushing victory will be within your grasp. Keep your artillery stacks to two units; this allows reserves to filter forward through the square to reinforce the front. I also like to advance most of my cavalry forward two squares at the commencement of combat. Although they tend to bear the brunt of combat and they don't receive a charge bonus during the second turn, it's still vital to maintain a row unimpeded by enemy influence to allow you to transfer your forces laterally to and from the flanks. Insure that you have a good mix of unit types on your front line. This maintains your offensive *combined arms* edge, and allows your cheap infantry to act as cavalry-shielding *cannon fodder*.

Finally, make sure you have good leaders; a leader who allows most of his subordinate units to attack has a significant advantage over his less experienced brethren; even when the odds aren't in your favor, a good leader can turn the tide. When you gain experience with your leaders, make sure you save those points up for leadership and attack improvements; you won't regret it.

SOME FINAL TIPS

Keep your eyes peeled for the enemy! Because your opponents move at the end of the game turn, you don't get to see their units moving across the map. If there's an enemy colony a stone's throw away from your capital, the first time you'll notice an invading army is when they're storming the walls (good design here)! Ships are also a problem, as the bigger ones have enough room for a veritable army on board. By keeping some frigates of your own patrolling the coast, you may be able to intercept and sink them before they unload their cargoes. Similarly, when you're shipping armies hither and yon, it's often a good idea to unload your troops when there are enemy vessels nearby at the end of your movement; you can always re-embark next turn and continue moving (assuming your transports survive).

Congratulations! You've now successfully established a foothold on the continent, your liege has sent you the nation's highest honor . . . and his treasurer is taxing the socks off you! Maybe you should declare independence? Maybe a trade agreement with the Dutch might be a good idea so you can off-load all that excess grapefruit? The rest is up to you!

12

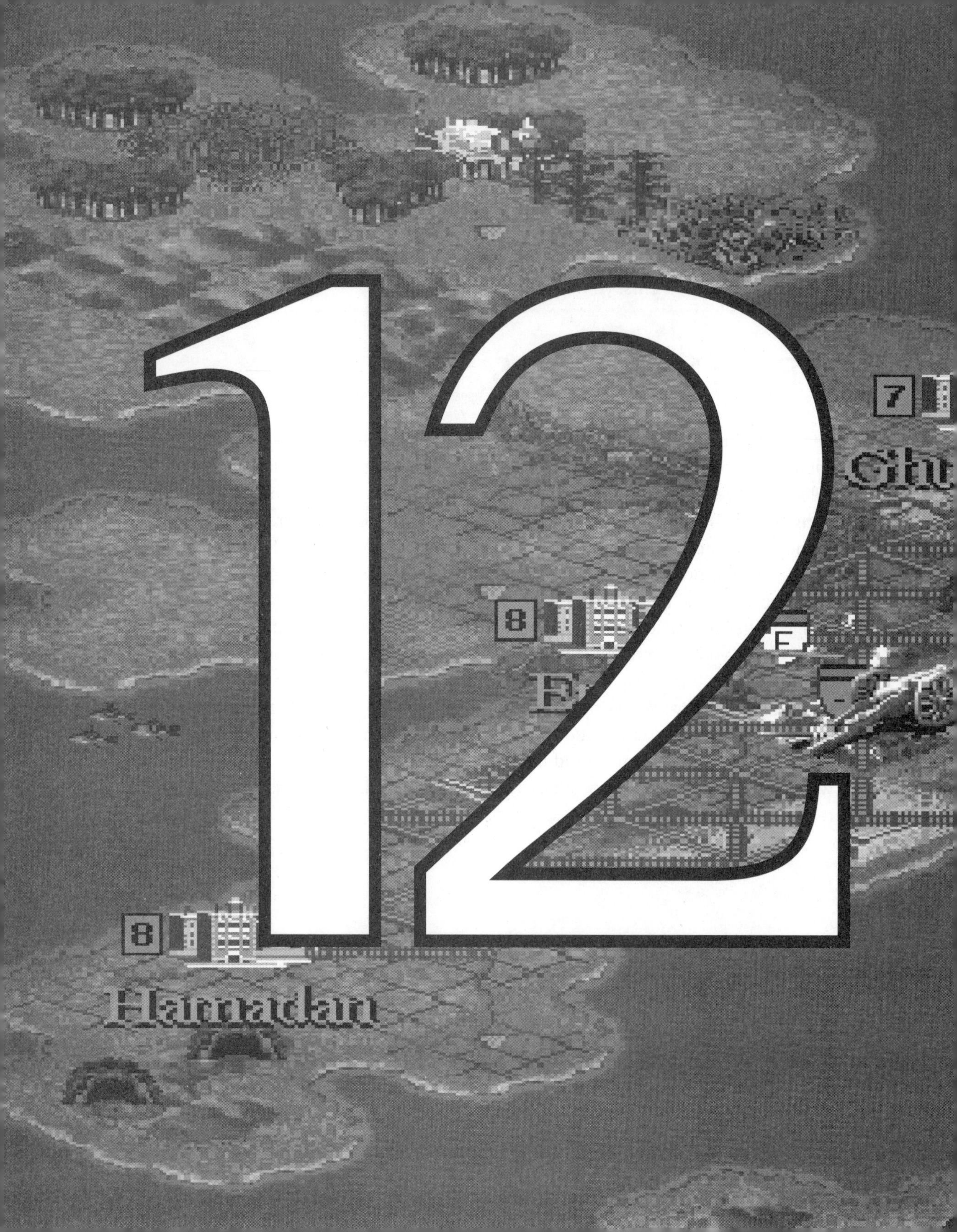

Battlegrounds

T his chapter presents strategy tips for a series of *Battleground* games by TalonSoft that allow you to recreate three historic battles: Gettysburg, Shiloh, and Waterloo. Prepare your troops for battle.

GETTYSBURG: WADING THROUGH THE HIGH WATER MARK

As befits a game simulating two very different armies in action, TalonSoft's *Battleground: Gettysburg* game plays differently depending on whose side you choose to serve. These differences play out most dramatically in the full three-day battle, in which the differences between the goals of the Army of the Potomac and the Army of Northern Virginia are clearest.

As the Confederates, you have to push hard and attempt to smash the Union force in detail to grab the high ground before the superior numbers of Meade's army begin to take their toll. As the Union, a stubborn delaying action is required to prepare the way for a proper defense of the hills and ridges south of Gettysburg, where Northern men and cannon can grind the Southern infantry into grits. Of course, knowing *what* to do is only half the battle; knowing *how* to do it can sometimes be a challenge.

Luckily, many of the tactical nuances of successful fighting apply equally to both sides. The Civil War occurred at an inopportune moment in the evolution of warfare, where the linear tactics of the Napoleonic age had lingered on into the world of rifled weapons. Consequently, the defense tended to have the advantage, as it was safer and easier to blast away from cover at people marching toward you than it was to march forward in the

CD-ROM
Check out the CD-ROM included in this book for the demo version of *Battlegrounds*.

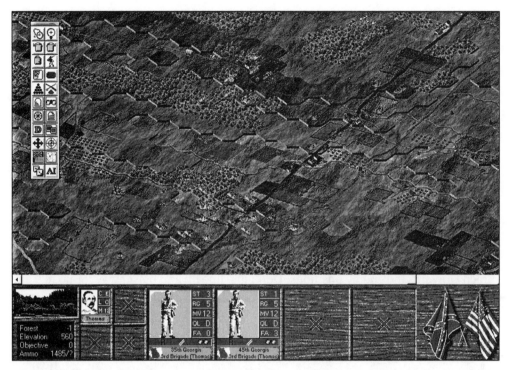

Doubleday's division comes in on the Southern flank, the hammer to the Iron Brigade's anvil.

open and blast at the same time. Artillery was largely a line of sight weapon, effective against masses of men but often inaccurate; gun crews were very vulnerable to rifle fire. Communication on the battlefield was problematic, usually devolving to shouts, flag waving, and frantic gesturing with predictably uncertain results. Both the North and the South had to deal with these aspects of war equally.

BE READY TO TAKE CASUALTIES

The basic concept to grasp is that you will take casualties, so make your casualties count. Expose your forces only when you have to. Your goal is to take objectives and kill the enemy, while losing as few men as possible. When you commit men to a fight, make sure you give at least as good as you get; for the outnumbered Confederates, you have to do even better than that. Go for enfilade shots, surprise assaults through the woods, and rapid marches around the enemy flanks. Overwhelm enemy regiments with a brigade, and brigades with divisions.

Don't fight fair. Use artillery *en masse*, pounding the enemy line while you advance to melee. Remember, every assault should end with a melee to seize the objective; everything you do should be aimed towards getting the most undisrupted men behind bayonets at the point of decision. A magnificent maneuver that doesn't bring your forces either into battle or onto decisive flanking terrain is wasted effort.

In *Battleground: Gettysburg*, leadership is fairly abstract; units do not need to be in command to move or fight, only to rally. The chief offensive problem, then, is how to get close enough to the enemy to drive him off of his position without taking unacceptable casualties. Speed reduces the amount of time in the kill zone, but the best speed is achieved using column formation, which in turn is terribly vulnerable to fire, especially from artillery (ten pins, anyone?).

Advancing in line is slower, but allows firing on the move and is somewhat less susceptible to fire. All you can really do is keep your assault troops under cover or out of range of the enemy until you actually start your attack. Then, move quickly and directly towards the enemy positions. Don't just line up and blast away for no reason; come out in the open and close with the enemy with the intent of ousting him from his positions.

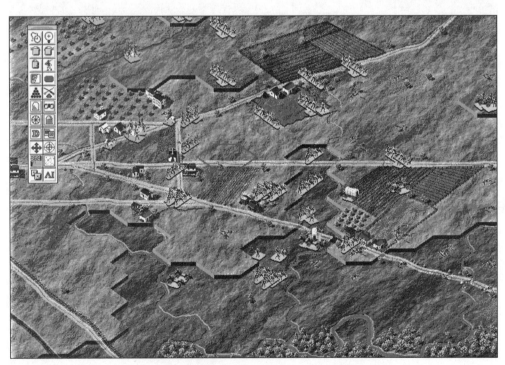

Concentrating on the point of attack makes short work of these Yankees.

Mass your regiments tightly in the assault, and keep a reserve brigade from each division if possible. Here too *Battleground: Gettysburg* is more lenient than real life; the game does not penalize players for concentrating 1,000 men in a hex, so there isn't much reason not to concentrate at the point of attack. Still, you will take casualties, which is why you have to have a reserve.

On the attack, the reserve can reinforce a breakthrough or exploit a hole you open; on the defense, reserves are vital to plug gaps in your line opened by enemy firepower. On the defense, you should spread out more to hold more territory. Keep whatever forces are not needed to hold the line in reserve, out of the line of fire. Plug holes in the line as they appear, and if you continue to take heavy casualties just standing there, move your line back and into cover.

RALLYING UNITS

Leaders should accompany the lead units of an attack as they close for melee, but otherwise should not expose themselves as they contribute nothing to fire combat. Take your routed units behind your lines with their leaders to rally in safety. When you get to the final push, however, your leaders should be with your regiments for that combat modifier, and to prevent mass routs. You don't lose any points if Gen. Reynolds takes a minie ball in the noggin, so when you have to win, make the generals earn their stars the hard way. Under normal circumstances, though, keep the higher level commanders safe.

Keep unit ranges and weapon types in mind as you plan. Most units are equipped with rifled muskets, which fire effectively out to five hexes. Artillery should never voluntarily move within rifle range of the enemy; use the guns' superior range to fire from a distance, and keep the close range firepower of grapeshot for those desperate defenses where you don't have much choice about the range of engagement.

Be very careful approaching carbine-equipped troops; Union cavalry and sharpshooters are deadly up close, as are most artillery units. Cover like walls and breastworks can help, but extensive close range fire will chew up the best of units. You might want to use poor quality but large regiments for fire support, as quality doesn't affect combat, and reserve your A and B quality units for close in fighting, where quality is important to avoid disruption.

BEAR THE GRAND STRATEGY'S BURDEN

As for grand strategy, the burden is on the South, but for both sides, the other army is the target. As the Confederates, you must attack. If the Union army is able to dig in on

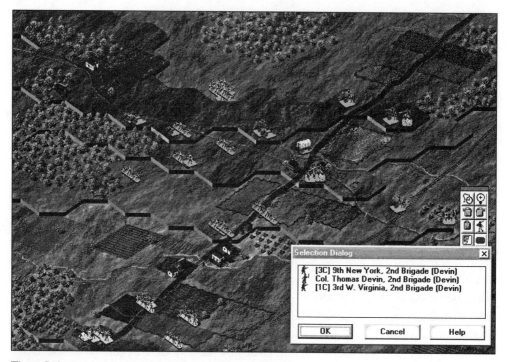

Them Rebs is sure smart, staying out of range of Union carbine fire; Southern rifles can shred Yankee horsemen at this range.

the hills and ridges south of town, Lee might as well pack it in and go home. The Army of Northern Virginia doesn't have the men to stand toe to toe with the blue bellies. What it does have is good troops, arriving fairly rapidly and in good position to out-flank the Yankees. Most of all, the Confederates have the initiative. The Union player, computer or human, has to react to Southern overtures.

With a little daring, you can force a division or two around the Union right and seize Culp's Hill on the first day, while Confederate cavalry harasses northern supply wagons on the roads leading north to Gettysburg. Move rapidly, but don't throw away men. If by the afternoon of day one the Southern side is inflicting more casualties than it is suffering, things are going well.

Keeping your divisions ordered, push the III Corps down the pike towards Cemetery Ridge, while II Corps closes in from the north. Extend your flanks as far as is prudent, to stretch the Union forces and keep them guessing. Behind the screen of your front line forces, bring up I Corps and center it behind the point you choose for

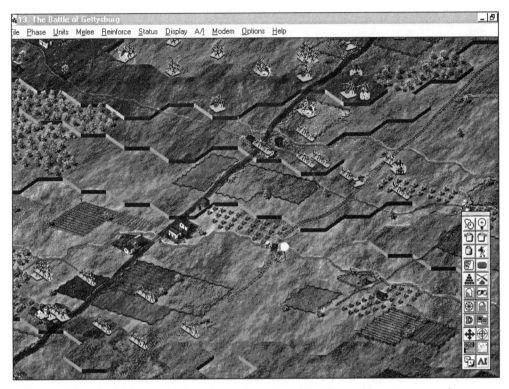

Putting artillery on hills to fire over your troops is something General Lee approves of.

your main assault. You don't have to throw it at the Little Round Top; you can crash straight through onto Cemetery Ridge or even onto Cemetery Hill itself.

The III Corps will usually lack the punch for a major assault after the first day, but II Corps will often have Rodes' division available for supporting I Corps. The key is to push hard, but keep your lines together. You have to push the Yankees off the objectives without allowing an opportunity for a devastating riposte.

The Union forces have some tricks to use too. Try to get the cavalry out of the battle as soon as possible. When Reynolds arrives, use the 1st Division to hold the line and withdraw Buford's boys; they give up too many points as casualties, and you can put them to good use observing and harassing the Confederate lines of advance. Likewise, think about bringing Doubleday's division in on the Confederate right. Mass your plentiful artillery on hills, firing over your riflemen and into the advancing Confederates. Push your reinforcements north and west of the town.

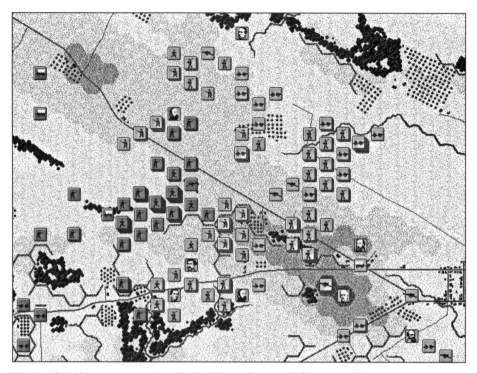

Moving fast, Lee manages to push the Union forces off Cemetery Hill.

The XI Corps will have to hold Ewell off for as long as possible, and should also detach a brigade or so to hold Culp's Hill. As night approaches, you should have positions on Cemetery Ridge and Hill prepared for your weary front line forces to fall back on. The longer you make the battle drag on, the better it will go for you. You can lose more men than the South, and you want to make Lee pay dearly for every yard of Pennsylvania countryside he takes.

SHILOH: WAR AIN'T FAIR!

To illustrate the danger of taking war game lessons at face value, this section presents some tactical tips for besting the AI in TalonSoft's *Battleground: Shiloh*. However, bear in mind that some of the tips for winning at *Shiloh* against the computer can result in disaster against a human opponent (let alone in real life!). Indeed, many of these tactics will work against the computer opponents in other war games; however, it's only the nature of the AI beast and current war game design that lets these tactics work.

THE DEEP RUN

The *deep run* is a name for the tactic wherein you send units (or, often, just a single unit) deep behind the computer's front line, either by punching through its lines or by circling way around its defenses to enfilade it operationally. Now, on the surface there's nothing wrong with this kind of tactic (can we say *blitzkrieg*?), but unlike reality, a small force (even that single unit) can often accomplish quite a bit against the computer. Some of these tactics will work against a human player, but usually because they cause this knee-jerk reaction: "Where did *that* come from?!"

TalonSoft games, like many war games, use the victory location as a measure of success; capture certain important hexes and hold them to gain points towards victory. Because these hexes can mean the difference between winning and losing, you should always keep an eye on them (especially when playing with fog-of-war on) lest they get taken from you without your noticing it. The computer opponent in *Shiloh* generally seems oblivious to victory hexes (especially to those far from its front lines), and you can often capture the hexes and then defend them with only a single unit; often you can even leave them empty.

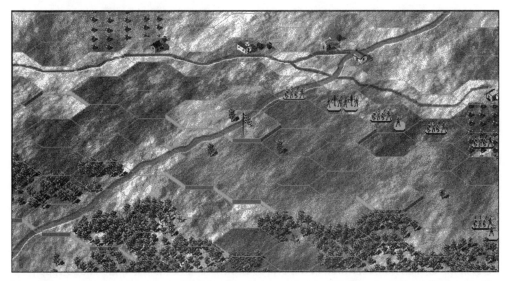

Note the victory objective just behind the Confederate line; seize it early and you'll often hold it against the computer the rest of the game.

For example, in the Prairie Grove scenario it's possible, early on, to punch through the computer's line to take the victory hex on the hill at 21,16. (Ironically, this was very similar to what happened historically.) There that unit sat for most of the rest of the battle. It would get fired on, but never heavily. It broke several times, running off the hill and away from the victory location. While waiting for the unit to rally, the Union-*owned* hex sat there, with the Confederate line just a couple of hexes away, completely undefended and ignored by the computer.

Similarly, a lone cavalry unit sent even deeper allowed it to capture both the victory hex at 13,23 and the lone supply wagon the computer leaves there. Leaving the hex undefended for the rest of the scenario, it was lost only because a *reinforcing* Confederate supply wagon happened to move along the road that passed through the site.

Several times a similar maneuver was performed in the Wilson's Creek scenario by sending a Union cavalry unit around the western side of Bloody Hill and down Skegg's Branch into the midst of the Confederate camp to capture the victory hex at

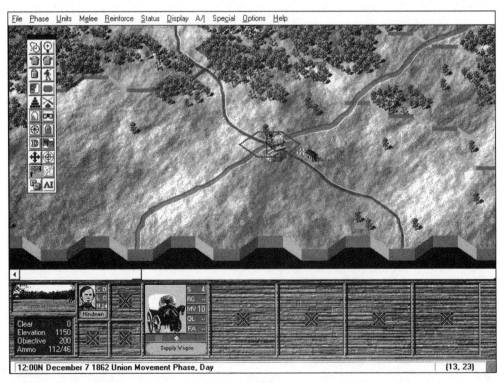

Deep in the Confederate rear area in the Prairie Grove scenario sits this undefended supply wagon and victory hex—easy pickin's!

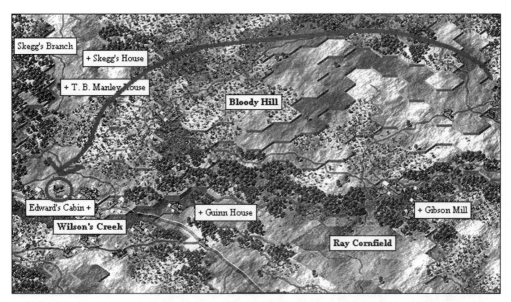

Performing an end run around Bloody Hill and directly into the Confederate camp, you'll likely lose the unit but can usually take the victory hex and capture or destroy a supply wagon.

19,11 and often capture or destroy the westernmost supply wagon. Of course, that unit is usually lost, but rarely does the computer bother to recapture the victory location, despite the fact that most of its units start out within just a few hexes of it.

You can also use the *deep run* tactic against the computer's intense defensiveness (for all things *except* victory locations). Playing the Confederates in Wilson's Creek, it's possible to tie up both of Sigel's artillery units at the south end of the Sharp Cornfield. During one play session one of the routed cavalry units (once it rallied) was sent around in an attempt to catch the artillery unprotected; because the unit was still disrupted (and remained so throughout the scenario), the artillery units could never be directly assaulted but were able to stay under fire for most of the game. True, there were heavy losses from the artillery fire that came from both units, but at least the computer was kept occupied.

A wise human player might initially panic upon having a unit appear in his or her rear like this but would not tie up a high-value artillery unit in an attempt to neutralize the threat (something you should keep in mind if an opponent ever tries such a maneuver on you).

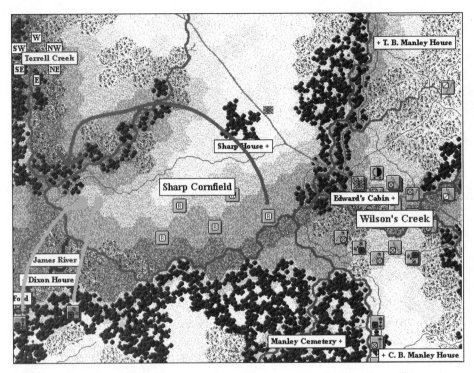

A lone cavalry unit can divert the attention of the computer, keeping its artillery units busy and away from the main part of the battle.

THE FIXED UNIT

Many if not all of the scenarios in *Shiloh* feature *fixed* units, units that can't be moved at the outset of combat. While perhaps frustrating, fixing units is a common if imperfect board game way of simulating surprise; *you* know you're playing a war game and, if you've played the scenario before or read details of a historical battle, you often have a pretty good idea of what to expect. In reality a commander was/is lucky to have even a vague notion of the enemy, and his forces were often caught (sometimes literally) with their pants down (the Confederates at Wilson's Creek and even more so the Union at Shiloh).

Hence, force a unit to stay in place until the period (roughly) when it moved historically. Fixed units in *Shiloh*, however, aren't completely frozen, a feature you might be able to turn to your (probably minor) advantage against either computer or human opponents. Fixed units start out in approximately their historical formations and facing; often you know ahead of time that these aren't the best and you can adjust them

to meet an enemy threat that's still some distance off, or prepare them to move or fire well ahead of their release turn. If they are in defensible positions, and you know you are on the defensive for the scenario, why not have them build breastworks?

Fixed units that are attacked before their release times are released immediately, and any units adjacent but not attacked will be released at the start of their turn (this in case your opponent does better than the historical figure). While the computer's fixed units will fire, they don't appear to adjust their facing or formation until they've been assaulted/approached. A wily gamer might be able to punch a hole through a computer fixed line (only *unfixing* two or three hexes' worth of troops) with a strong column (especially in the woods around Shiloh, where the still-fixed units only a hex or two from the head of the column may not be able to see your activities).

An even sneakier (and more unrealistic trick) is to *fire on your own fixed units*; while this may result in some casualties it will also release all the units in the fired-upon hex. Obviously, you'll want to use the smallest unit possible—it only takes one to *loosen* a stack—to lessen the damage to your units (direct artillery fire is not recommended!); the Union player can try to use indirect fire from the gunboats because such fire doesn't generate casualties, but it also doesn't always *wake up* a target hex.

If you're in a real hurry to develop a big force, you can have fixed units in a row fire one after the other at their neighboring stack (a lead-heavy tap on the shoulder). The result may be a (probably very) slightly battered force that can be brought quickly into play; this tactic will always work against the computer, but should only work once against a human opponent. (But what a surprise it could be!)

MAP EDGES AND OTHER BOUNDARIES

Map edges are a wholly unrealistic feature all too common in most war games, but they make for wonderful defensive terrain—no design I've seen allows for units to maneuver off the map and back onto it, and only the smaller battles like Wilson's Creek or Prairie Grove tend to be small enough to fight the battle with plenty of maneuver room to spare. (Although even here a retreating enemy can be backed up against a map edge and annihilated, giving you a better score than if the enemy could retreat off the map as actually happened at Wilson's Creek.)

Use the map edge as an impenetrable anchor for your defensive line (but be careful not to anchor it at an enemy reinforcement point; incoming units may automatically destroy your units sitting on the entry hex). On the offensive, use map edges as an anvil to smash the enemy against; with a map edge at the enemy's back (or, even better, on two sides) it takes fewer of your units to effect an encirclement, so when the

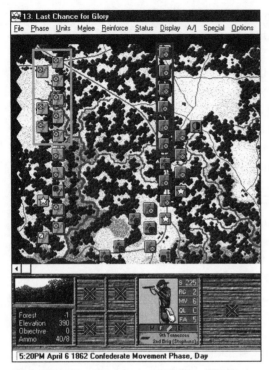

Unit positions at the start of the "Last Chance
for Glory" scenario.

result of your assault on the hex is retreat for the enemy the units will be destroyed
instead.

EXPERIMENTATION IS KEY

Once you've played a game engine through a few times, you'll begin to discover such
tricks (often just stumbling on them). If you have an idea, put the game into hotseat
mode and experiment; there are many tricks not covered here, and surely many more
waiting for you to discover. Just don't complain about weak AI if you actually use any
of them!

WATERLOO: AVOIDING THE PLUNGE

TalonSoft's third battleground entry covers one of the most studied battles in history—Napoleon's final effort to reestablish himself as the leader of a French-led European community. This game offers a series of scenarios, culminating in the battle in its entirety. However, one should resist the urge to plunge into the complete battle scenario, as the smaller scenarios lead one to lessons learned that can improve the potential for an ultimate victory.

One may micromanage each and every battalion under one's command, but this ultimately becomes overkill. The more logical command method is to carefully husband one's resources, achieve a breakthrough, and then allow the subordinate commanders to reassert control. At Waterloo, Napoleon failed to assert personal charge; at Arcola, twenty years previously, he had done so and achieved victory. The player should be prepared to do likewise.

Most of this section is devoted to the French, since they bear the burden of changing the status quo. The British win by maintaining their position; the French must decisively defeat Wellington before he and Blucher can join their armies.

THE STRATEGY

Historically, Waterloo represented the French strategy of the central position. An attritional element of warfare, it lacked the minimal casualties incurred by the indirect

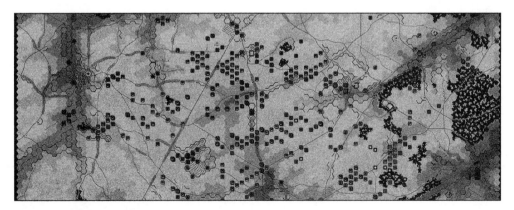

Waterloo—End of the Battle

approach. However, Napoleon's army at Waterloo in fact lacked the finesse of the *Grand Armee* of 1805, and brute strength was called upon to substitute for both strategic and tactical finesse.

Initially, one should not allow the Marshalate to assume control. Ney's abilities may have been permanently damaged by the Russian Campaign, and the Emperor himself characterized the Marshal's comprehension of Napoleonic strategy as that of "the last joined drummer boy." Thus an abysmal artificial intelligence may in fact represent the abilities of Napoleon's main subordinate.

An examination of the battlefield itself reveals that the British line is overbalanced towards the west. While this is fine for allowing a linkup with the Prussian forces, the British Army is thereby rendered vulnerable to being cut off from its supply line and the sea. One might assume that a threat against the British right flank would cause a massive shift in British forces. Historically, Napoleon did not seriously threaten the right and in game terms, the threat does not alarm the computer-led Anglo-Allied forces.

In game terms, one must break the British strength through the center. This can be accomplished by assaulting the British allies; the Dutch and Belgian forces are easily fatigued, and do not have the staying power of the British first-line forces. Judicious assaults against the center when combined with flanking movements against the British left flank can often serve as the keystone to victory. As the center is weakened, it becomes vulnerable and the French can often split the British line in two.

When playing any scenario, make sure that the victory conditions are understood. Terrain can yield the victory, and one should not become distracted by easy kills. Just as important is the element of time; as the Emperor noted, "one has a limited time for war." Note the time span of scenarios, and attempt to map out the likely positions of one's units in future hours. Optimal plans that run out of time for proper execution are succinctly referred to as *defeats*.

THE TACTICS

Attempting to learn hard-and-fast rules for employment of the Napoleonic arms is an exercise in frustration. Terrain, time, and the nature of one's forces and opponents can force one to adapt tactics in an ever-changing milieu. There are certain *most-likely* rules of tactical employment:

1. If infantry is the queen of battle and artillery is the king of battle, then enemy infantry skirmishers are the hemorrhoids of battle—they are a

pain in the butt, are difficult to remove, but it is such a relief when they are finally gone! Actually, Waterloo seems to overemphasize the strength of the skirmisher formation. Use them as often as possible, and try to destroy the enemy's skirmishers as quickly as possible. When assaulting chateaus, maximize skirmisher stacking in the adjacent hexes. While this would historically have proved vulnerable to enemy artillery and massed fires, the casualties will not be as high as expected, and this is the only method to seize the fortified hexes.

2. The standard rule for the employment of cavalry is *don't!* While the British historically feared the French lancers (as more of a psychological threat than an actual combat threat), the same is true in game terms. Cavalry exerts a threat zone of six hexes, and it is usually more efficient to use the cavalry as a morale/fatigue deterrent than as an actual combat-committed unit. Once the cavalry is committed to a charge, it quickly becomes disordered and vulnerable to counterattack. Even successful cavalry charges often become Pyrrhic victories. Therefore, when you are tempted to use cavalry, stop and reconsider. If you still feel that the cavalry is called for, stop and reconsider once again. Only after this

The French Cavalry charge British square.

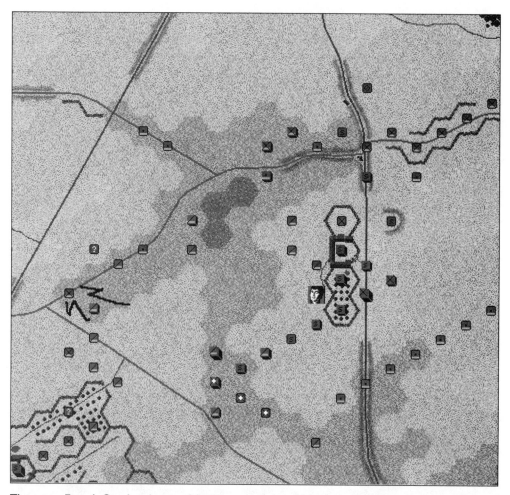

The same French Cavalry charge of British square, but in the two-dimensional perspective.

second consideration should one be willing to commit to the charge. The only exception is for employment against routed troops; the cavalry does an excellent job of slicing and dicing already-routed forces, and this yields quick victory points. Just make sure that the enemy riposte is not overwhelming. If enemy skirmishers are in the open, they are a valid target for cavalry, but do not send the cavalry into the woods after skirmish formations.

3. Artillery is dangerous but not decisive. In fact, based upon repeated play-ings, my personal feeling is that the artillery is not as effective as it could have been historically. But massed fires, especially against formed troops (particularly large infantry square formations) yield a cheap and tempt-ing target. On the other hand, chateau/fortified hexes seem invulnerable to artillery fire, and the lack of a reconnaissance by fire option renders the artillery as more of an also-ran than it should be.

4. Infantry formations are situation-dependent. Strangely enough, both line and column formations can stand up to cavalry assaults until fatigue ren-ders them overly vulnerable. Knowing when to change from line to col-umn and vice versa is a fine art which can often become obviated by the battlefield. Disordered troops cannot readily adjust their formation, which means that those troops most in need of change cannot achieve it. One faces a conundrum—column formations allow one to close with the enemy with minimal disorder from terrain, but are more vulnerable to enemy fire. Line formations allow more efficient use of firepower, but one can rarely march in line formation without becoming disordered. Try smaller scenarios and use the French mixed order-flank battalions in col-umn and interior battalions in line. However, this was a rather subtle combat formation, and at Waterloo, massed columns were often employed. Of course, the player is not as restricted. As a rough rule of thumb, enemy infantry fire at a distance of two hexes is unlikely to be decisive, but adjacency yields effectiveness.

5. Prussians are slow and stupid. As they make their presence known on the French right flank, they may be bottled up and delayed with minimal effort. Judicious use of skirmish formations, cavalry, and artillery can force the Prussians to deploy in the woods where they tend to mill around. When the pressure increases to the breaking point, trade space for time. To show how fearful the Prussian formations are, they will cease their advance and deploy when faced with unlimbered artillery—even artillery that lacks ammunition! Use their weakness to the maxi-mum advantage.

6. Know how to employ supply wagons and leaders. Running out of ammunition in the midst of battle is not an inducement to high morale.
   Similarly, know that troops will break, and be prepared to rotate them in
   and out of the main line of resistance so that they may freshen up and
   become less brittle.

THE GAME MAP

Waterloo has the feel of a miniatures battle. Its 3-D aspects encourage the user to employ
the "normal view." This has the beauty of being enmeshed in the action, but the dis-
advantage of becoming unplayable. In the normal 3-D aspect, one does not lose the

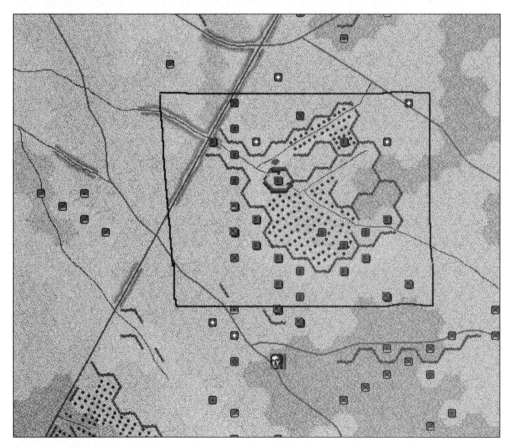

Assault on Hougomount in the two-dimensional perspective.

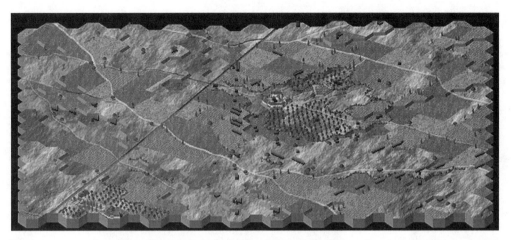

The same assault on Hougomount as above, but in the three-dimensional perspective.

forest for the trees, one loses the trees for blades of grass. Even the 3-D zoom-out (the default) has some of this danger, and one should be prepared to view the map in both two- and three-dimensional perspectives. The two dimensional views are akin to the standard war game, and resemble SPI's board game *Wellington's Victory*. But one cannot utilize the two-dimensional aspect alone because its portrayal of facing is much weaker than that of the 3-D modes. Therefore, use the two-dimensional aspect to gain strategic appreciation, and use the three dimensional aspect for tactical engagement.

For those who have succeeded in decisively defeating Wellington and Blucher, take heart. An additional 400,000 Austrian, Russian and South German troops are marching to engage. While some historians feel that a Napoleonic victory at Waterloo would have caused the dissolution of the latest coalition, it is more likely that Napoleon would have eventually had to surrender to what were becoming insuperable odds.

The assault on Hougomount in extreme zoom.

13

Rome

3 Tar

Ne

alis

Lilybaeum

Caesar II

Though *Caesar II* might aptly be described as "SimRome," anyone who's played it will soon realize that unlike *SimCity*, *Caesar II* is a very demanding game. Aside from the obligatory barbarians, there are lots of ways for you to fall off track and run your city into the ground: rioters, economic woes, and disease are nothing to be sneered at. Still, *Caesar II* is manageable if you develop a good initial strategy. Just remember to save early and save often, because this is one of those games where one sudden, unexpected incident can ruin your whole career.

GAME SETTINGS AND FORUM SETTINGS

The first thing you should do when you start the game is reduce the speed to zero. Some people think it's better to let time pass as they build the city slowly, but this isn't necessarily so. If you freeze time while you outline the skeleton of your city's roads and water structure, you'll be less likely to make rushed decisions and critical oversights.

Taxes are a vital part of your economic survival. The tax rate on businesses and homes begins at 5 percent. Leave the taxes alone until you have a fairly successful city, with land values in the 20s and 30s; then increase it slightly, but not too much—maybe just a point. It's best not to increase the tax rate beyond 7 percent, and seldom beyond 6 percent, because tax-induced riots are *really* a nuisance.

CD-ROM
Check out the CD-ROM included in this book for the demo version of *Caesar II*.

Conscription is a very touchy subject as well. It starts at a meager 2 percent, which yields you very few soldiers. Gradually increase the rate to 4 or 5 percent, if you're feeling lucky.

The Plebeian forum is very important. Increase your Plebe spending to 30 Denarii from the start, just to get enough Plebes to cover your basic services and start your army off on the right foot. You should have the recommended level of Plebes in every job, plus 100 in the army—though you can get away with fewer soldiers in a peaceful province.

THE CITY LEVEL

When you begin a new city, set the game speed to zero. Now survey the terrain. It's best to build a city in the curve of a river; that way, water will always be close, limiting the need to build expensive aqueducts. Don't expand on both sides of the river, though; keep it to one side, so you can use the river as a natural wall if you try to build city defenses.

Draw the outline of your city by creating a road network, and a water network including reservoirs and fountains. Avoid using wells, since fountains are cheap and much more desirable.

You'll soon find that sprawling cities, though quaint, are incredibly tough to maintain. Building a city skeleton out of three or four 10x10 squares of road is a much more manageable size. Because road access extends three squares from the road itself, a house put anywhere inside of that 10x10 block will automatically have road access, unless it's in one of the four central squares. Plunk a bath house down on those four squares, and all the residents of that block now have bath access. This is a great way to efficiently provide basic road and bath coverage for everyone.

Now that your city skeleton is set, you need to add some other basic features. These are the services many players consider most vital:

* Bath houses
* Markets (2 per 10x10 block)
* Prefectures (2 per 10x10 block)
* Hospital
* At least 2 temples
* At least 1 business
* At least 2 theaters for baseline entertainment

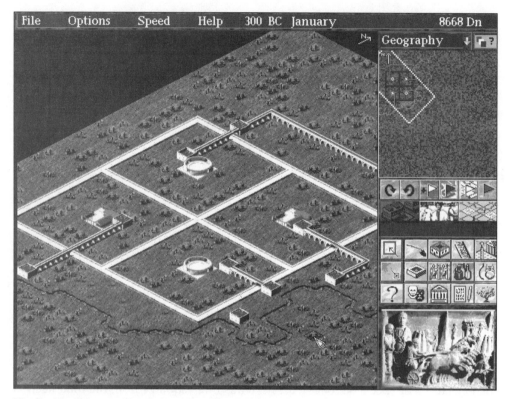

Here's the skeleton of a city based on 10x10 blocks.

If you can put all these things into your city before you crank the game speed back up, you're in good shape. Where should these structures be placed? Well, roads and water are already taken care of; we'll tackle bath houses later in this chapter. Prefectures should be placed *outside* the city blocks. Run one square of road out from the main city block and stick the prefecture at the end of it. This ensures the prefecture will protect the block, but will also be distant enough from the housing that its negative effects won't be felt. Speaking of distances, the following table presents some important distances to bear in mind:

DISTANCE SPECIFICATIONS FOR CONSTRUCTS	
BUILDING OR CONSTRUCT	**SERVES POPULATION WITHIN X SQUARES**
Road	3
Baths	5

BUILDING OR CONSTRUCT	SERVES POPULATION WITHIN X SQUARES
Market	Variable: needs direct road access to housing
Aventine Forum	Depends on roads (up to 8 squares)
Market	Depends on roads (negative impact within 2 squares)
Prefecture	Depends on roads (negative impact within 2 squares)
Grammaticus	6
Rhetor	8
Theater	5 for full impact, 9 for lesser impact
Business	Doesn't matter (negative impact within 4 squares)

A general guideline to follow is that entertainment facilities (Theater, Odeum, Arena) should be in the middle of your city blocks so they can spread maximum contentment. The same holds true for educational facilities (Grammaticus, Rhetor) and, to a lesser extent, religious structures (Shrine, Temple, Basilica). Prefectures, markets, and businesses should be placed outside the city block and connected by a short length of road (usually 1 to 3 squares). This keeps the populace shielded from the negative effects of these structures.

Now fill two of your 10x10 squares with housing; leave the others for future expansion. If you build too many houses, you'll end up with a big, low-value slum and lots of disease, because a big population requires several hospitals.

Once the city is set in motion, watch the Oracle closely, especially the Culture rating. The comments in that area are often vital. If your city has lots of markets and businesses, good land value, and all the necessities of life, you will often find that your houses aren't growing, or worse yet, they're shrinking. The Oracle can tell you whether lack of temples, entertainment, or city services is the culprit.

Certain areas of housing will not flourish, and there will always be one or two squares that just don't seem to take off. Destroy these and replace them with shrines, plazas, or gardens, though Shrines are usually best. Shrines boost the quality of the land all around.

Most games are won or lost on the City level. The key is to provide basic services from the very start, in the locations in which they do the most good, and then provide extra services only when they are needed. It's very easy to build too much housing, too many roads, or too many entertainment facilities, and before you know it you find yourself going into debt. Try for a small but profitable starting city; then slowly build on it when it begins to support itself. Only later should you worry about city walls; rather, you need to stop barbarians before they get into your city.

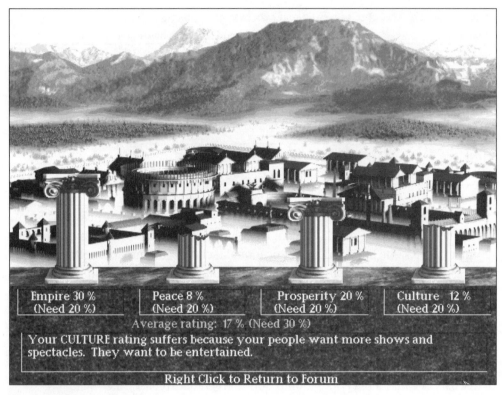

Empire 30 % (Need 20 %)	Peace 8 % (Need 20 %)	Prosperity 20 % (Need 20 %)	Culture 12 % (Need 20 %)

Average rating: 17 % (Need 30 %)

Your CULTURE rating suffers because your people want more shows and spectacles. They want to be entertained.

Right Click to Return to Forum

Check the Oracle often.

THE PROVINCE LEVEL

Don't build much on the Province level when you're in a new territory. Some provinces are very compact, so you can connect several towns with a minimum of road.

Most provinces are sprawling expanses, though; you shouldn't worry about connecting everything. For starters, you need one industry (a farm, mine, or quarry) that's connected to your city by a road, a Cohort Fort to house your soldiers, and a road connection to the nearest neighboring province. If there are no adjacent provinces, a Port is necessary. If you can connect some little towns to your main road easily, then do so. Otherwise, leave them for later.

When you get some excess wealth, build a second industry. It is very possible to generally squeak by without ever building a trading post or a second fort.

These installed shrines replaced destroyed cheaper houses.

COMBAT

Combat in *Caesar II* is very straightforward, and you can even make the computer fight for you. Overall, there isn't much to it. Still, here are a few salient tips.

You need an army comparable to the barbarians if you're to win a battle. Don't even *try* to fight unless the numbers are close. Once you do enter combat, line up the slingers in back and protect them with light infantry in the Tortoise formation. This lets you get maximum use out of your slingers, because the Tortoise formation lets the infantry protect them for a long time as they rain stones upon the heads of the heathens. By the way, combat is far too hard to manage at game speed ten. Seven is much more manageable, yet isn't so slow as to bore you to death.

If the barbarians attack a little border town, just let 'em take it, and then build up your army and take it back. If they attack your main city, you can delay them by building two or three sections of wall right in their path. They are too dumb to go around

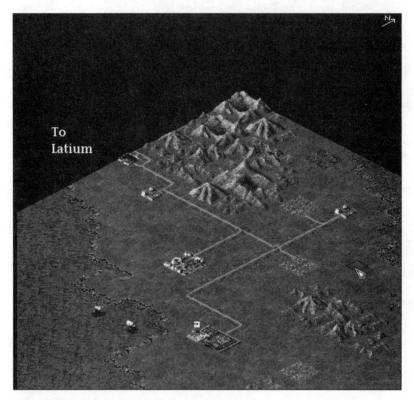

Don't try to connect the whole Province at once.

it. I know, I know . . . this isn't too realistic. But do you know what? It works. If things start to go badly, you'll need every dirty trick you can get your hands on. Good luck!

A LESSON IN
ANCIENT CITY MANAGEMENT

As you fire up the system, crack your knuckles, and pull the *Caesar II* CD from its case, you can't help but ponder that ages-old question, "What exactly is the difference between a Roman governor and a galley slave?" The difference (besides a lot of paper-work and staff meetings, or, alternatively, a lot of whips and heavy rowing) is *money*. Cash. Denarii. Dough. Dead emperors. Moolah. Enough of it, and your city prospers.

This is a sound combat formation—infantry in front and slingers in back.

Too little, and you'll be sharing an oar and a set of leg-irons with Uglius Maximus, the guy too mean to throw to the lions.

Why is this? Well, let's just say that the Emperor may want you to believe that he is a patient and forgiving sort of monarch, but this is an outright lie. He's shallow and greedy. And if you don't make your city profitable, he'll be more than happy to hand your little province over to somebody else. After all, he has at least a dozen more fawning sycophants just like yourself, all of them waiting for you to make a mistake. Needless to say, you don't want this to happen. But how to prevent it? When you're starting your first city, it's difficult to make a profit at first.

SPEND MONEY TO MAKE MONEY

Well, as they always say in those get-rich-quick seminar videos you see advertised on late-night television, you have to spend money to make money. And, fortunately, you start out the game with a certain amount of cash. This will be very useful in setting up your main source of income: industry. You may dream of fine palaces, plazas, and arenas. Visions of armies and conquest may dance through your head. But it's a good idea to put these ventures on hold until you're making enough cash to support them, or else you'll find that your startup money disappears faster than donuts left unattended in the programmer's break room at a software game company.

So this leaves you with the practical question of how to start out that first city and not lose your shirt doing it. Well, if you're playing the game in City mode, part of the work is already done for you. The game assumes that you have a stable supply of raw materials from the surrounding province. If you're playing in Province mode, however, you'll have to set that up for yourself. If your province has access to either a land or sea trade route, you'll probably want to set up a trading post or a port. Although these are more expensive to build than farms, quarries, or mines, you don't need to hire plebes to work there. This makes ports or posts a one-time investment, instead of something which has to be maintained monthly.

Place several warehouses around your port or post, and build a road to the city. If you have access to more than one trade route, you may want to build an additional port

Industry is the foundation of your city. Build it first.

or post so you can bring different types of materials into your city. This is a good idea because you can only use so much of one type of material. Once the warehouses start filling up with raw materials, you can return to your city and build factories to turn the stuff into something that your fellow Romans will actually want to buy.

Probably the most important thing to do once you go to your city is to safeguard that startup money. It's rather difficult to build profitable industries, or anything else, when some thief is three provinces away, spending what used to be your treasury on wine and loose women. And it's even tougher to explain the situation to your Emperor. Place some temples and shrines in a block in your city. Nobody safeguards your money better than priests. This fact has some historical basis, because the first Roman mint was built in a temple. For extra protection place several prefectures around your block of temples. This will provide soldiers and guardsmen to patrol the area. For high-security or industrial areas you should place the prefectures 6 to 7 spaces apart to make sure that you have complete security coverage.

GETTING THE PEASANTS TO WORK

Now it's finally time to build those factories. Unfortunately, however, you can't just plunk the factories down and expect them to turn out products on their own. Although the Romans made staggering technological advances in the fields of agriculture, irrigation, and sanitation, they just didn't get around to inventing the fully-automated assembly line. So you're actually going to have to persuade some Romans to move to your city and work in the factories. And the one thing that you need to know about these Romans is that they are, by and large, pickier than the average Persian cat. If you don't keep them happy enough, they'll move away, or riot, or set your city on fire, or even go whining to the Emperor about what a bad governor you are. And that's a one-way ticket back to that ocean cruise with Uglius Maximus that we mentioned earlier.

The most dangerous Roman complaint is "We're thirsty!" Nothing inspires more hatred in the hearts of your little virtual citizens than the lack of fresh water. Although you could just sink wells and provide a primitive water source to an area, you'll make your Romans much happier if you provide them with running water. This means you'll need to build a system of reservoirs and aqueducts to carry the water from the river. If you place your reservoirs 13 spaces apart you will have complete piped water coverage of an area. Piped water, however, is only half the battle. You will also need to build fountains, to bring the water to the surface. This is where the Water detail map comes in very handy. Place your fountains so that all of the areas you plan to develop have both piped and surface water available. It's also a good idea to place bath-houses next to your reservoirs because this helps to improve Roman morale and to reduce the risk of plague.

Now that you have a water supply, there are a few more things you'll need to complete your Roman Industrial Park. For example, it's rather difficult for you to make money off of your factories unless you have somebody there to collect taxes for you. Build Aventine forums 6 to 7 spaces apart to provide complete tax coverage for the area. You will also want to place markets within 6 spaces of your factories because they won't produce anything if there's nowhere to sell it. Finally, you'll want to connect everything with roads. Road access is essential to commerce in your Roman city. Some structures, such as markets, forums, and factories, have to be touching a road in order to be able to use it. Others, such as houses, can be one space away from a road and still have access to it. If road access is not available, most buildings will be considered inactive. A factory without a road won't produce anything except cobwebs.

Build housing close to your factories.

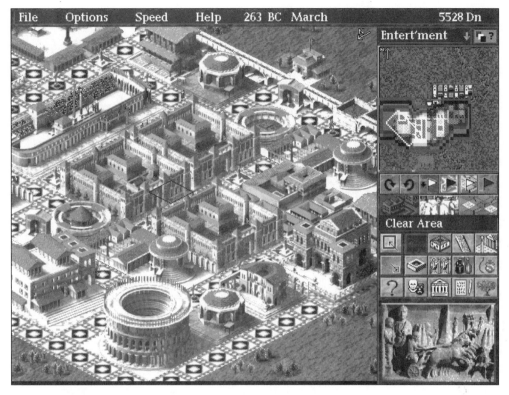

Your new neighborhood . . . if you're lucky.

One useful trick here, if you're playing on Novice or Easy level and have extra cash to spare, is to build plaza squares instead of roads in your industrial area. Plaza squares are counted as roads, plus they also tend to raise property values in an area. You'll find this to be very important because the presence of a factory makes the local property values drop faster than the resale value of a '72 Pinto. As a matter of fact, you can guarantee that your factory district won't exactly be the high-rent section of town. And because Romans don't like to live in low-rent areas any more than you do, you can expect unrest in your industrial quarter. So it's a good idea to liberally sprinkle the area with prefectures. Build them a space or two away from any housing developments because prefectures also lower property values.

And speaking of Roman housing, you're going to need to build some. The houses need to be relatively close to your factories because your little industrial guys don't like to commute very far to go to work. After all, the two-car family is still a couple of millennia away.

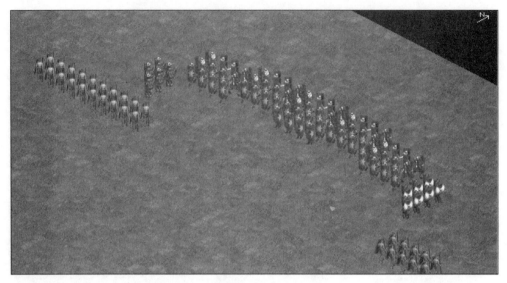

Save that world conquest for later in the game.

TIME FOR EDUTAINMENT

That's it! Now that you have your industries set up you can turn the rest of your startup cash into public works, education, hospital facilities, entertainment, housing for you and your well-to-do friends (on the other side of town from the meat-packing plant, naturally), and, of course, that army that you've always wanted.

Oh, there are two final things that you may want to know. First, and most importantly, never ever ever forget to bribe the Emperor. Little things that might otherwise annoy him (such as a slightly unprofitable year, a bad harvest, or a 27 block riot in which his statue is pulled down and smashed) tend not to bother him quite so much if his pockets are well-lined with your money. And once you start bribing him, he'll be even harsher on you if you stop. So don't. Second, make certain that you hire more than enough plebes to take care of your city. If you don't have enough of these hard-working guys, it's a toss-up whether the city will burn down or fall apart first.

In future years, as long as you don't spend more than you make, you can expand your city, develop your province, increase foreign trade, and take over neighboring tribes for fun and profit. So good-bye and may you have a long and happy rule, successful conquests, and a life free from Mr. Maximus and all his shipboard friends.

Hail!

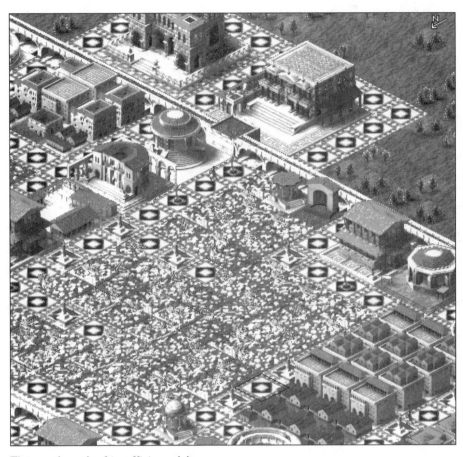

The usual result of insufficient plebes.

Battle Isle 2220—with its 60-plus weapon systems, 40 scenarios, and modem/network play—is chock full of tactical and strategic possibilities. There is not a single unit that has the best of everything—if it seems like it does, then it moves like a snail, costs an incredible amount of resources, or its caliber or armor is low. You almost always need to use all units at your disposal. If you think you can ignore that new transport helicopter, or if you think it's boring, well, you'll need it to surprise attack your opponent with a paradrop or to fly over a river without a bridge (and otherwise impassable).

THE LOW DOWN ON THE ISLE

An oddity of *Battle Isle 2220* is that you neither see the computer move its units nor do you see combat during the AI turn. Although it may seem like it, your units are not mysteriously destroyed during the turn as if some Dune–like sand creature swallowed them whole. After holding your breath while the turn bar slowly progresses and counts up the casualty figures, take a few moments to assess what damage you took, who killed which of your units, and where the AI moved. Look for experience increases and possible presence of hidden artillery for unexplained high casualties. You should also look at the chart listing units destroyed during the turn.

CD-ROM

Check out the CD-ROM included in this book for the demo version of *Battle Isle 2220*.

RECONNAISSANCE—THE ENEMY WENT WHICH WAY?

Your recon units are your *antennae* for your main body of units. Protect your antennae—it doesn't take much for the enemy to whack them right off. Use recon to understand the layout and flow of the battle. This will help determine whether you should be attacking or bracing to receive an attack. Don't let your units conduct suicidal recon by advancing short-sighted units into unexplored territory. When this occurs, your enemy gets first shot, making this an expensive tactic. It's like running down a dark corridor screaming "banzai!" The enemy will surely know you're there and will wallop you senseless.

You can use some of your secondary or damaged units to spot for you at unlikely avenues of attack or to use as a red herring in a diversion. By tricking the AI about where your actual intentions are, it may divert a bulk of its forces like jackals to carrion.

These opportunities don't come often. A group of ammo transporters await their destruction by the surrounding armored vehicles.

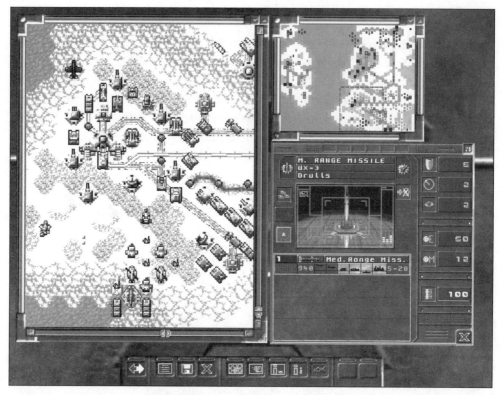

Access rear areas by using helicopters to drop units near valuable targets. Here units in the south attempt to take out a UX-3 and two ammunition transporters.

If you have a large monitor, use high resolution (1024 x 768) to show more of the map and displays. You can use one of these displays, the top five display, to get some information on what the major enemy units are that you may not have encountered yet. It also shows how many of the best five units are yours, giving you a partial indication of your relative strength.

MOVEMENT—YOU CAN'T GET THERE FROM HERE

Traffic jams: they're bad in real life and bad in this game. Don't pile up along a road. Send units to road flanks to advance and reconnoiter. If you have some units that are not an integral part of your battle plan, don't just take them along for the ride. Use them as flank or rear-area guards, keeping them off congested roads. If you are working with an ally (AI or otherwise), keep a path free for his units. Watch out when

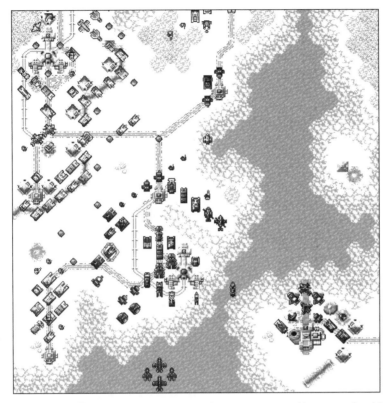

You can use Fortresses to transport units across water. Here you should conquer the SW city and then take out the mines with long range attacks.

transporting units because they will suffer damage when their transport is hit, should they survive at all.

There is no *undo* movement option, and sometimes one mistake can blow an entire mission; so save often, unless you have lots of time and patience on your hands. As you shuffle your units around, ever so cleverly, be aware of range restrictions on some units such as the Archimedes rocket launcher, which is capable of hitting targets five spaces away. It's easier, it seems, to be aware of maximum range and not minimum range. Archimedes rocket's cannot hit targets less than three spaces away. What a frustrating feeling when you realize you have nosed up too close to your target!

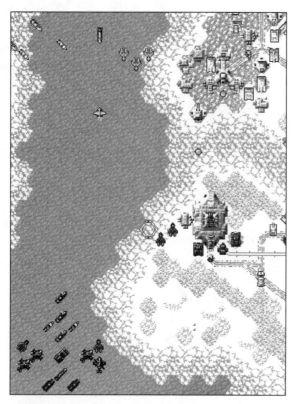

An air/sea battle is brewing. Advance your planes and ships along the coast to protect your HQ, which also has a handy AA gun mounted on its roof.

PRODUCTION/REPAIR—TIME FOR A LITTLE R & R

Remember, repairing units, while detrimental to experience, is cheaper in terms of energy and material relative to buying a whole new unit (not to mention a new unit is green). Don't be in a rush to build units and commit them piecemeal. Resist building cheap units just because you have the resources— the materials and energy won't disappear. Wait a turn or two to afford a unit that may fit better into your overall strategy. Also, take into account the speed of the unit and/or if it has transport. It may take several more turns before it arrives at the front—even more for an advancing front.

Although the manual says units will lose experience if they repair or refuel, this is not the case. Repairing, indeed, will remove an experience point, but refueling will

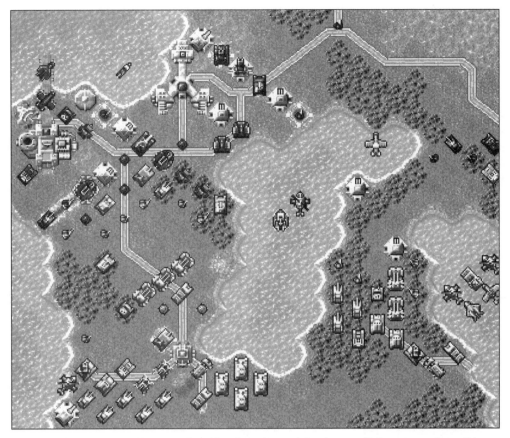

Use trenches, mines, and geographical bottlenecks to defend yourself. Be aware of possible beach landings and paradrops.

not. It makes sense not to lose points for refueling, whereas repairing introduces inexperienced men to the unit so the loss of experience is appropriate.

ON THE ATTACK—THEY CAN PUT IT TOGETHER BUT WE CAN BLOW IT APART!

Move units, even ones that you won't be using for attack (weakened/low ammo), next to targeted units to increase your odds due to hex control. This will take advantage of the debilitating surround effect even if you have no intention of attacking with the surrounding units. Planes and long-range weapons should be on your list of priority targets.

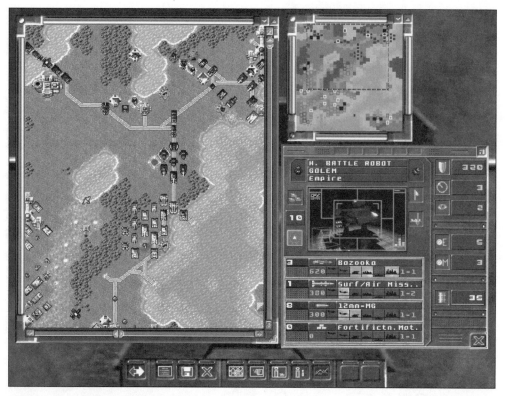

Delay your attacker until you can amass a proper force to counterattack. Use your Golems to build trenches and destroy roads.

If you get an early warning that a particularly strong unit(s) is approaching, don't always rush up to engage it. Hold back to gain experience through some nearby skirmishes. By then, he may just be arriving to the battle, saving you the fuel and time. Summarily attempt to destroy him in a concerted attack. When you do attack, try to make sure you can follow through. If you are going to spend the time, ammo, fuel, and health of your units on weakening enemy units, you should finish them off as soon as possible. Otherwise, they may be repaired, allowing them to haunt you in later turns.

Taking a building is just half the fun; sometimes you get captured units as well! Keep an eye out for enemy units that are heading to recapture buildings or to repair, and try to time your capture appropriately. Make sure you protect your building—capturing capable units—especially when you have sent out a small attack group to take a remote area. Losing such a unit is costly in terms of time and opportunities, if

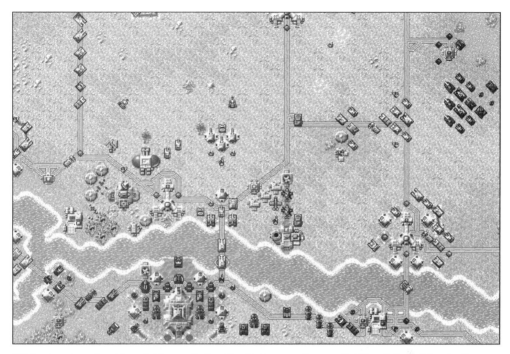

NE tank group should assist in capturing the factory on the north side of the bridge to the south. Without it, you won't be able to replace lost units.

you need to send out another to replace it. In the meantime your opponent may have sent additional forces to the area, making conquest more difficult.

ON THE DEFENSE—LET 'EM AT US!

Sometimes enemy units are initially placed on your flanks. Avoid committing all your units to the front. Keep a reserve in the rear area for defense and possible emergency or opportunity deployment.

Many counterattacks, perhaps obviously enough, start when you take an objective. Placing some fixed defenses around a newly captured building will help your defense, if the AI sends units to recapture the area. When contemplating a retreat, bear in mind that some units must move around entrenchments. This may buy you some time and allow focused attacks against obvious avenues of approach. Consider destroying roads or blowing bridges. It takes a good amount of firepower to destroy it, especially with inexperienced units. Keep track of damage done to each road section; otherwise, you

The Flying Fortress is capable of many things—blowing this bridge to smithereens is one of them.

may forget which one you've been targeting. Assess how the demolition is proceeding; there might not be enough time to blow a road, depending on available firepower. Ideally, a demolition unit will be available, making short work of the road.

Don't hold a line just to hold a line—retreat, especially if you aren't giving up any objectives. Keep movement speeds in mind if your unit is trying to escape destruction. If it is slower than its pursuers, then maybe it would be better to use the unit to side-track your opponent. Send it off away from the front lines, away from some of your more sensitive units, or use it to check out possible enemy staging areas. During your turn don't forget about your fixed weapons—turrets and pill boxes. Because they are not units that are part of the move and fire procedure, you may occasionally miss the opportunity to use them, if you're not paying attention.

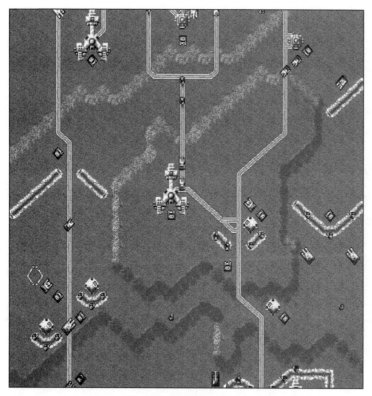

The enemy sometimes has fallback positions available. Notice the empty entrenchments in their line of retreat. Try to get behind units before they can reach these positions.

EXPERIENCE—WE WEREN'T MANUFACTURED YESTERDAY, YOU KNOW

Early in the campaign, the missions will provide your units with the necessary experience to become nasty killers later in the campaign. Track each unit's experience and give units that have long-term importance to your war effort first crack at earning experience. Also, make sure a seasoned unit at maximum experience isn't doing mop-up work. This *wastes* experience and the unit should be saving its ammo for more serious threats.

Take advantage of the fact that you get one star for each battle—take two turns or so to destroy a non-threatening unit, or have several nearby units take secondary weapon shots so that they all get experience. Beware, however, of boosting a

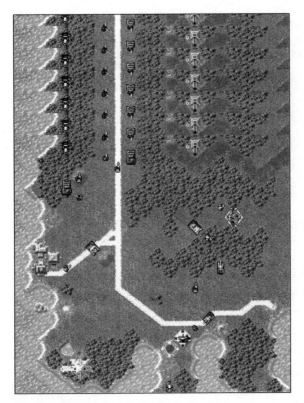

You can deploy robots to key areas.

formidable enemy unit's experience by jabbing it with numerous ineffectual attacks. Keep in mind units receiving ranged attack will not get experience points. Because it causes loss of experience, make sure you have sufficient resources to fully repair a unit—do it once and do it well. Making multiple minor repairs will drain valuable experience.

GENERAL STRATEGIES—IT SEEMED LIKE THE RIGHT THING TO DO AT THE TIME

Don't use main guns to eliminate an opponent if secondary weaponry will do. Exploding ten Sting missiles into a group of Atlas transports makes for great animation but wastes good ammunition. In general, try to use your short range attackers that have limited targets first, and then more flexible units can be deployed to finish off units or assist in your choice of local battles.

If you think you probably won't be able to safely carry away a crystal, don't simply give up and let the enemy take it. One option is to simply destroy the crystal with weaponry—if you can't have it then neither should he! Another option is that sometimes it's worth it to attempt to pick up a crystal because, in a worst case scenario, your unit is destroyed (make sure you have a replacement handy), but you've also kept him from obtaining it.

For some additional insight on AI tactics use the cheat codes shown in the following table to reveal an entire map on normal or difficult level. Type **ewald** and press F9 the first time; continuing to use the cheat codes requires only pressing F9 thereafter. You will see German codes on the screen, so the English translation is listed in the table.

CHEATS

# GERMAN	ENGLISH	EFFECT
1. Mission fortsetzen	Continue mission	Does nothing
1. Mission gewonnen	Win mission	Makes you immediately win the mission
1. Mission verloren	Lose mission	Makes you immediately lose the mission
2. Unit nicht auffüllen	Unit not resupplied	Does nothing
2. Unit auffüllen	Unit resupplied	Refuels and re-arms the unit under the cursor
2. Unit entleeren	Unit emptied out	Empties out the unit under the cursor
3. Erfahrung nicht ändern	Experience unchanged	Does nothing
3. Erfahrung 0	Experience to 0	Changes the unit under the cursor experience to 0
3. Erfahrung 4	Experience to 4	Changes the unit under the cursor experience to 4
3. Erfahrung 8	Experience to 8	Changes the unit under the cursor experience to 8
3. Erfahrung 10	Experience to 10	Changes the unit under the cursor experience to 10
3. Erfahrung 11	Experience to 11	Changes the unit under the cursor experience to 11
4. U–Boote nicht sichtbar	Submarines not visible	Makes all submarines invisible in the map window (default)
4. U–Boote sichtbar	Submarines visible	Makes all submarines visible in the map window

(Continued on next page)

(Continued from previous page)

# GERMAN	ENGLISH	EFFECT
5. Anzahl nicht ändern	Number unchanged	Does nothing
5. Anzahl 1	Number 1	Changes the unit number under the cursor to 1
5. Anzahl 5	Number 5	Changes the unit number under the cursor to 5
5. Anzahl 10	Number 10	Changes the unit number under the cursor to 10
6. Aufklärung nicht ändern	Visibility unchanged	Does nothing
6. Alles aufgeklärt	All visible	Makes all of the map visible
6. Nicht alles aufgeklärt	Not all visible	Restores normal visibility
7. Computer an	Computer on	Computer controls the non–human players (default)
7. Computer aus	Computer off	Makes the player controls also the computer players
8. Besitzer nicht ändern	Ownership unchanged	Does nothing
8. Besitzer übernehmen	Ownership changed	Makes the human player control the unit under the cursor (includes enemy units)
9. Alliierte nicht ändern	Allied unchanged	Does nothing
9. Alliierte steuern	Control allied	Makes the human player control the allied army (this feature has a shortcut: type *bauer* during play)
9. Alliierte Computer	Computer allied	Makes the computer control the human player allied (default)

Source: Battle Isle 3: Unofficial Home Page (http://www.studionet.it/andrea/bi3.html)

Watching the AI in full view will provide valuable knowledge on it's strengths and weaknesses in various scenarios and situations. Using the additional cheats shown in the following table will allow you to experiment with all kinds of *what if* situations. To help you with individual scenarios, there is a list of mission objectives hidden at the very end of the game's readme file. Time to return to battle, so sit back and flex your mental muscles. Factum!

Cheat Menu

☐ Mission Fortsetzen
☐ Unit nicht auffüllen
☐ Erfahrung nicht ändern
☐ U-Boote nicht sichtbar
☐ Anzahl nicht ändern
☐ Aufklärung nicht ändern
☐ Computer an
☐ Besitzer nicht ändern
☐ Allierte nicht ändern

This is the cheat menu, which you can access by typing *ewald* and pressing F9.

CODES FOR INDIVIDUAL MISSIONS

#	MISSION NAME	CODE
1.	The Pretorians	2975462
2.	The Advance	6487674
3.	The Ships	1564386
4.	The Landing on Kaar	9745642
5.	Battle for the Factories	3756838
6.	The Aircraft Corporation	2957843
7.	The Two Kai Factions	8844366
8.	The Drullian HQ	2375411
9.	The Expeditionary Force	3854653
10.	Urelis	5647332
11.	Kol–Lorz in Danger	4092664

(Continued on next page)

(Continued from previous page)

# MISSION NAME	CODE
12. The Supply Lines	7564366
13. Skom	8264241
14. The Tank Wedge	3243554
15. Terdon	5487436
16. The Battle for Skom	1353411
17. The Port of Magalo	4524338
18. At the Gates of Hallwa	6731244
19. In the Capital City	1243371
20. The Final Battle	6245425

Heroes of
Might and
Magic

Heroes of Might & Magic (henceforth *Heroes*) is an excellent strategy game in the same vein as the venerable *King's Bounty*. A game of tactics and careful management, *Heroes* lets you play a variety of scenarios or attempt a full-scale campaign.

Instead of focusing on the nuances of each individual scenario or part of the game, this chapter will outline some of the soundest strategies for *Heroes*, and point out some game mechanics that will help you regardless of what scenario you're playing. Following strategy and tips, some basic design points will be covered to help you design your own levels.

BEGINNING GAME STRATEGY FOR BUDDING HEROES

In *Heroes* you take control of several, um . . . *heroes* who roam the land with their bands of monsters, taking over castles and resources and battling other heroes. Your champions never participate directly in a fight. Rather, their attributes enhance the performance of their armies (i.e., the hero's defense score is added to his units' defense rating). The hero can also cast spells and make key tactical decisions—like retreating!

THE MECHANICS OF THE GAME WORLD

CD-ROM
Check out the CD-ROM included in this book for the demo version of *Heroes of Might and Magic*.

The heroes themselves are relatively cheap to purchase, and you can buy an unlimited number of them at your local castle. As they gain artifacts and experience their ratings increase, and their forces become increasingly powerful.

Therefore, remember this: a low-level hero is completely expendable, while a high-level hero should be guarded with care. It takes time to build up a high-level champion, and fresh-faced recruits can always be replaced if you have a couple thousand gold pieces. It's the armies that are hard to replace, not the low-level heroes.

Around the landscape you'll see four basic types of structures and objects: treasures, castles or towns, enemies, and resource-generators like sawmills and mines. Treasures should be picked up if convenient, enemies should be ignored if a fight isn't profitable, and resource-generators should only be captured if it's convenient or necessary. The problem with a sawmill or a mine is that unlike a town or castle, it cannot generate troops to defend itself. If you want to defend it, you'll have to keep a hero nearby, but that's a waste of a hero. Instead, capture those buildings when they happen to be nearby, and don't worry if they're stolen by enemy players. When you run short of a particular resource like gems, wood, or mercury, then go out and recapture the appropriate building.

Towns should always be turned into castles as soon as possible; when you get control of a castle, you should build every single structure that you can (with the possible exception of the Thieves' Guild). Most of these structures produce troops, and you'll soon find that gold is fairly easy to come by—but only a few troops are generated each week, so they're a little harder to accumulate. Therefore you want as many buildings generating troops each week as you can get your hands on. Furthermore, the very last structures you're permitted to build produce the best troops (like Paladins, Dragons, or Phoenix). High-level troops are infinitely preferable to low-level units in *Heroes*.

Why is a high-quality unit consisting of a single, 200 hit-point Dragon better than a group of 200 Peasants with 1 hit point each? It's inherent in the way combat works. Let's say you send your 200 Peasants into a rough fight and just barely win. You've secured a victory, but you've also lost almost all your Peasants—maybe there's 20 or 30 remaining. Your Peasant army is reduced to a tiny brigade, and is essentially useless. However, let's say that instead you send a single Dragon into that fight. If the Dragon wins the battle, it emerges without a scratch because damage doesn't carry over from battle to battle. So your Dragon is still in great shape, ready for another fight. That's why big, high-toughness creatures are worth your while; they'll stick around for the long haul, and you won't have to keep buying replacements.

Aside from their good toughness and attack power, most big creatures have bonuses that make them extra handy. For example, Hydras attack all adjacent spaces, Trolls regenerate, Dragon and Cyclops attacks span two spaces, and Phoenixes and Dragons can fly over walls and have excellent overall mobility.

GAME STRATEGIZING

Your game will often be won or lost based on how you spend your first 20 or so turns. If you are slow to start, your power base will not grow along with those of your enemies; you'll find that even when you defeat the enemy heroes several times over, their superior resources will allow them to rebuild their armies faster than you can destroy them. So plan carefully when you first start to play!

Here's a formula that has worked pretty well in most games:

1. Grab the Loot

You start the game with a single hero. Send him out to circle the castle and pick up any loot that's easy to reach. Capture any buildings that happen to be nearby. Figure out the limits of your surrounding area. Most games start you out in a fairly enclosed locale; if you want to escape, you'll have to kill the monsters guarding the mountain passes and paths through the forest.

While your hero is looking and exploring, you should make sure to build a new structure in your castle every single turn. Don't forget and waste a turn. Almost all buildings are useful, but if your hero has poor spell power (i.e., if he or she is a Knight or Barbarian) you can save the Mages' Guild for last. Ignore the Thieves' Guild completely.

2. Build an Expeditionary Force

Once your hero has investigated the immediate locale, he should return to the castle and get as many creatures as he can from the newly built structures in the castle. Yes, this leaves your castle open to attack, but in most scenarios you have a little time before the enemy gets close. Obviously, if you start out with bad guys swarming all around you, you'll need to leave a garrison at the castle.

The hero should now take his newly formed army and destroy the weakest monsters in the immediate area, like hordes of Peasants and Pikemen. Target the monsters who guard artifacts and treasures. When you find treasure chests, by the way, it's almost always best to distribute the gold for experience points instead of keeping it; remember, gold isn't that easy to come by.

If you can help it, don't attack the creatures who guard paths into or out of your little area. Leave them for now—they'll act as a buffer to deter enemy units for awhile.

You should still be building up your castle; at this point, you'll have almost every building. The very best buildings sometimes require resources you don't have, like

Mercury or Crystals. Remember which resources you need, and keep an eye out for buildings that produce them.

3. Restock the Army and Roll Out

Send your hero back to the castle. Some more troops should have been generated by this time, so give 'em all to the hero and send him away (once again, if enemy units are nearby, leave a garrison). Create a new hero to guard the castle; a castle without a hero has a tough time warding off attackers. The mere presence of a hero (even a low-level one) tends to discourage attacks.

Your older, experienced hero should now start to explore the territory farther away from your starting castle. If he can explore overland, by all means have him do so.

The main concern here is to conquer another town or castle. This provides you with both another source of revenue and another source of troops. If you fail to acquire a new castle in the early stages of the game, you'll have an extremely hard time matching your enemies' armies later on. So snag that new castle, and if you capture a town instead, make sure to turn it into a castle as soon as possible.

4. Fortify the New Castle

Your experienced hero should now sit at the new castle until you've repeated the building process you just completed (or nearly completed) at the old castle. Leave him there to guard the place until you have constructed as many buildings as possible and created a decent-sized garrison to defend it, and maybe give the hero some fresh units for his army. When the new castle has been thoroughly fortified and garrisoned, the experienced hero can leave once again for more exploration. At your discretion, you may now purchase a third hero to sit and guard the new castle.

5. Gather Supplies and Continue Expanding

Now your experienced hero can continue to explore, take over new castles, and take over new supplies. You'll find that wood and ore—especially wood—run short as the game goes on, because so many buildings require those elements. Take over mines and sawmills whenever possible, as well as any miscellaneous resources you might need.

Eventually your older castles will build up big enough garrisons that they no longer need their heroes to defend them. At that point the heroes defending the castles are free to roam the countryside and explore, conquer cities, and recover artifacts. Make sure to keep bolstering your old garrisons, and you'll be well on your way to victory.

A final bit of strategy involves the options menu. Make sure to leave "View Enemy Movement" enabled, and leave heroes' movement at a fairly slow speed so you can really see what the bad guys are up to. That way you'll know immediately when your castles are under-fortified, because the minute your heroes leave you will see enemy troops making a bee-line for them.

POLISHING THE GEM

The strategic game in *Heroes* is predominantly about economics, building up armies, and deploying those armies, to deprive your enemies of the ability to do the same. On the strategic level, your military goal is to bring the enemy to battle on your terms. The tactical game is where you fight those battles and put your strategic planning to the test.

SOME MORE STRATEGIC GUIDELINES

Several basic guidelines can help you succeed at the strategic level. The first is, *kill armies, not cities*. In *Heroes* capturing a city does no damage to its component structures, or to the losing player's treasury. If you lose a city, you can just take it back. Losing *armies*, however, is much more painful. It can take weeks to replenish a good tack of high value units. So, if you kill your foe's troops, over time her cities will fall into your lap.

The second rule of good strategy helps you implement the first: *build few, strong stacks instead of many weak stacks*. Only heroes can command armies, so every army you send out will have a hero. A weak stack is just gargoyle fodder and a great way to lose a leader.

By building strong stacks, led by leaders with good stacks and magic items, you can deploy powerful, survivable forces. By picking your armies carefully, and using magic, you can maintain enough mobility to compensate for having fewer forces in the field. Start the game with good combat leaders like knights and barbarians; finish with warlocks and sorcerers, or build up those bully boys with magic items.

Always protect your economy while disrupting that of your enemy. Collect the loose piles of gold and resources near your starting city, and anywhere else you travel. Never miss a chance to swoop by a mine or laboratory. Transferring money and resources from your foes to yourself is a good way to win the war. This means protecting your resources, and that's tough.

Generally, use strong stacks with dimension door capability and a good hero to *patrol* an area rather than static garrisons. The enemy doesn't usually attack castles that are strongly garrisoned, but what you think is strong is probably just an appetizer for that marauding warlock. Garrisons strong enough to really deter an attack are better used with heroes in the field. If you have to garrison a castle, use a stack with a hero, so you can bug out if necessary.

Except in "find the widget" scenarios, where speed is vital, play it safe. *Build up slowly, and wait for the enemy to make mistakes.* Pick off heroes who stray too close to your domain, and expand gradually using a killer stack or two. Win in a day, in a year, it's all the same. You need to explore, of course, but avoid pitched battles unless you're sure you can win. When you do need speed, ignore most everything else. For instance, in Scenario 3 of the campaign, you have to find the Eye of Gorus; the first to do so wins. That makes your priorities clear: find obelisks, and find the Eye. Build only enough to support your heroes and keep you in the game. If you dally, you'll find yourself bowing to some other hero who moved faster.

Capture your new home; don't build it! As for buildings, despite the need for good intelligence, thieves guilds are not very useful. By the time you build enough guilds to give you an accurate and useful picture, there are often only one or two opponents left. Besides, you can get better intelligence from spells, which give you great strategic and tactical information when properly used. As mage towers provide many other magical benefits as well, your resources are generally better used building them than constructing haunts for highwaymen.

BUILD ARMIES EARLY AND MAGIC LATER

In the beginning, a good stack of trolls and ogres is awesome; by the end of the game, you will need to toss meteor showers and teleport spells about with abandon. It costs too much to build mage towers early, but you will need them later. As the really useful combat and non-combat spells only come with level 3 and level 4 towers, you can't skimp. Make sure that your best leaders have good spell casting abilities, via magic items and experience. And concentrate your magic items, too; it's better to have one leader with +10 to attack than three at +3.

Strategy is only a way for you to bring tactics into play effectively. Getting to the battle is half the problem. You can set up a relay of heroes to shuttle armies across a continent, however, if you plan correctly. Start with the troops you want to move under command of a hero. Move the cursor over the next hero in line; you should see the

double arrow symbol that indicates an exchange order. Now it's time to move. Once the first hero gets to the second, swap off the troops to that second hero, then move that second hero to an exchange with a third, etc. Once you acquire good magic skills, however, the best way to get the fire brigade to the fire is the trusty dimension door spell, used repeatedly. Two or three casts will cover a lot of ground, and leave you with enough mobility to attack the stack you just appeared next to.

Once you get to the battle, you should fight smart. Use combined arms. Fast troops allow you to strike first; heavy troops absorb damage well. You need missile troops to win consistently. Your ranged weapons serve two purposes. First, they draw enemy fire like fire hydrants draw Dalmatians. The computer players will *always* attack the most dangerous missile units you have. You can use this to your advantage, of course, by attacking the attackers from their flanks. Second, your missile troops can devastate many enemy stacks before they ever get into range. Of course, if your troops fall victim to enemy spells or raiding gargoyles, you'll have to have the back up of powerful armies with lots of hit points. A good hero with a defense bonus really helps protect missile troops.

BUILDING UP MAGIC

Though weak at first, *magic is crucial*. Build up your magical powers until you can teleport, toss lightning, and cast meteor showers. Use the lightning on single strong stacks and the meteors on a cluster of weaker units. The following table lists spells by level.

SPELLS BY LEVEL

SPELL	TYPE	LEVEL
View mines	A	1
Bless	C	1
Curse	C	1
Dispel magic	C	1
Protection	C	1
Slow	C	1
Teleport	C	1
Summon boat	A	2

SPELL	TYPE	LEVEL
View artifacts	A	2
Anti-magic	C	2
Blind	C	2
Cure	C	2
Haste	C	2
Lightning bolt	C	2
Turn undead	C	2
Identify hero	A	3
View heroes	A	3
View resources	A	3
View towns	A	3
Berzerker	C	3
Fireball	C	3
Paralyze	C	3
Resurrect	C	3
Storm	C	3
Dimension door	A	4
Town gate	A	4
View all	A	4
Armageddon	C	4
Meteor shower	C	4

Teleport spells are great for airlifting your Cyclopses or Hydras behind enemy lines, where their sudden appearance will no doubt cause dismay. Haste is another vital spell, as it makes slow units like Ogres much more effective. And resurrection is great for top-end creatures like Dragons and Paladins; just be sure to cast it before the battle is over, as you can't resurrect outside of a fight. And don't forget the old berserker ploy; cast this on a unit in the midst of your foe's host and watch the fun begin. Just make sure you cast berserk on a unit that hasn't moved yet, or you'll just waste the spell.

KEEP TROOPS HOMOGENOUS

Do not mix troop types; these folks just don't mix well. You have four basic types of troops: plains, forest, farm, and mountain. With only one type of troop in an army, the morale bonus is +1. Two types is neutral, but three gets you a –1 penalty, and all four types nets you a whopping –2 on morale, guaranteeing that your troops will freeze and panic in combat. It makes no difference what the *alignment* of the hero is; any hero can lead any group of armies. See the following table for alignment averages.

AVERAGES FOR ALIGNMENTS

ALIGNMENT	GROWTH	HP	SPEED	ATTACK	DEFEND	MINIMUM DAMAGE	MAXIMUM DAMAGE	COST
Overall average includes top unit in each group (i.e., all units that you can produce).								
Overall average	5	37	2	7	6	5	10	465

For each alignment that follows, the first line is the average of all units; second line is average without the top unit.

Average Farm	6	22	2	7	7	4	7	253
w/o Paladin	6	16	2	6	6	3	5	184
Average Forest	4	34	3	7	6	6	12	475
w/o Phoenix	5	20	2	6	5	3	6	270
Average Plains	5	32	2	7	4	5	8	338
w/o Cyclops	6	23	2	6	3	3	5	256
Average Mountain	4	59	3	7	7	7	14	793
w/o Dragon	5	31	3	6	6	3	6	352

Nomads, genies, and rogues don't seem to have any alignment, but they make it impossible to get the +1 bonus for having a homogenous army. If you make sure to grab every morale and luck bonus you can before you fight, your one-alignment army will have a great advantage in combat; just watch your Paladins take four lucky swings, and see whose standing in the end.

It is especially important that heroes who depend on magic have durable escorts. Nothing is as frustrating as having your high-level Warlock with a zillion spells driven into exile because his escort of two Archers and a Peasant was zapped by ten Sprites and an Elf. Always remember that *leaders only support combat; they don't fight.* They are important, however, so don't be afraid to run away. Surrender, if you can afford it, or just flee, if it looks certain that you are going down for the count. This is especially true if your hero is very experienced, or has many nifty geegaws with her. After all, you gotta be alive to be a hero!

BUILDING NEW WORLDS

When New World Computing released *Heroes* in 1995, it was something of a sleeper. Moderately priced, inconspicuously packaged, it slipped onto the shelves and into gamers' hearts as one of the surprise hits of the year. About the only thing this fantasy strategy game lacked was a scenario builder and a facility for randomly generated games. With commendable speed and perception, New World has remedied these shortcomings with the Windows 95 version of *Heroes*. Still priced under $40 in most stores, this revision delivers 16 new scenarios and a capable editor along with seamless Windows operation. An upgrade option, for $15, is available for owners of the original game who want to get graphical.

While the new scenarios are welcome, it is the editor that makes this version a must buy for fans of the original fantasy free-for-all. In essence, you can do two things with the editor: generate random maps or create custom scenarios for yourself and others. To facilitate creating random maps, the editor provides an option to generate a map and save it without revealing its contents, thus preserving secrecy. To assist in creating custom worlds, there is a healthy selection of editing tools and devices to aid budding weltmeisters. Still, the editor is not quite as easy to use or as flexible as the one in SSG's *Warlords Deluxe*, nor as slick as the one in MicroProse's *Civilization II*, and takes some getting used to. Creating random worlds is simply a matter of setting sliders and clicking on a button, but making your own scenario takes a bit more effort.

A THEME FOR ALL WORLDS

As in all creative endeavors, it is generally best to have some idea of what you want to create before you start. A general theme or strategic situation is good . . . once you clear all of the extraneous bits (check the clear all box on the erase screen).

DETAILS, DETAILS

Editing the details is a bit easier. While the standard drawing tool is a bit coarse, by holding down the Shift key you can edit/place individual squares. The Control key and a click places a 2x2 block, which is actually the smallest block that can stand alone. Between these techniques, you should be able to refine your map to your satisfaction. A little bit of patience should yield some rather smart looking continents in relatively short order. The only hitch is, if you have an irregularly shaped grass island and you

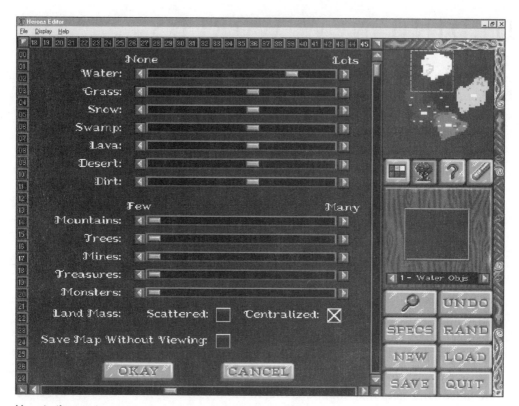

Use similar settings to generate a good starting template.

want it to be a large snow island, you have to start from scratch, and redraw the rough rectangle and cut and smooth out the shape you want. You can't just overlay snow on grass, for example, as drawing with terrain types replaces everything under the box with, you guessed it, another box of the new color. So, make sure you draw your initial continents in the type of terrain you will ultimately want them to have.

Next you need to give your map some topographical relief and geographical detail, as in mountains and valleys and forests and rivers. Each terrain set—grass, dirt, snow, swamp, and lava—has its own group of features, though most are simply variously colored versions of an archetypal shape. Mountains and forests generally run NE/SW or NW/SE, though you can do horizontal and vertical barriers if you're careful.

There are a number of single-cell, or square, pieces as well, to fill in gaps, and an extensive collection of knick-knacks such as fountains, shrines, oracles, statues and fairy rings in addition to the usual array of productive terrain such as mills, mines, and laboratories. Note the perspective that *Heroes* uses; it is easy to miss the fact that

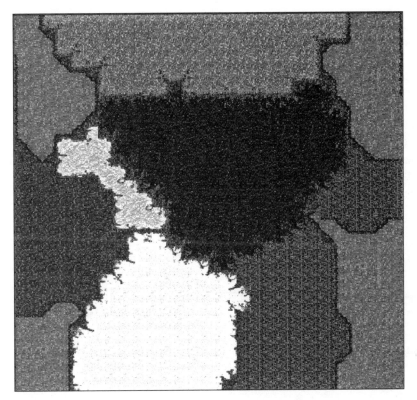

The world after randomization . . .

you can place terrain behind many objects. The red outlined base of an object can't overlay another, but the green outlined part can. Thus, you can fill in gaps between mountain ranges with an assortment of pine trees, for instance, to give a better look to your hillocks. Likewise, be sure to use the zoom feature to take a peek at what your map looks like up close; basic editing should be done zoomed out for speed, but fine work requires a more detailed look.

The crucial thing to remember about *Heroes'* terrain is that much of it is impassable. Mountains and forests are absolute bars to normal locomotion, while only boats can traverse open water. To confuse things a bit, the single square trees are not barriers, unless clumped together in 2x2 blocks. Teleport arches or spells can zip you about, of course, but aren't always handy.

When designing a map, be sure to allow your heroes access to all parts of the map, unless your intention is to channel movement. A small pathway through the mountains or forest will do; try not to make the routes too tricky to spot, as the computer

. . . and after clearing the unwanted details. Now, you can begin!

won't have any problem in finding the correct way even if humans will. Impassable terrain is very useful in designing maps, as it determines the boundaries of expansion and can help pace the game.

For instance, if you want your heroes to develop their realms without much contact from abroad early on, hem them in with mountains and forests, and force them to develop boats or teleport spells in order to see the world.

Another approach, one used extensively in the game's existing scenarios, is to guard pathways between realms with big stacks of monsters; this is a good trick, and can lead to interesting strategies such as suckering your neighbor into weakening those dragons so you can take them out.

Resource allocation is tricky. Too little, and heroes wither away; too much, and there's little challenge left. One good approach is to decide on the overall level of

If you don't want trespassers, you have to overlap your mountains and forests.
This barrier is hero-proof.

resources you want—rich, moderate, or scarce—and then decide how you want them distributed. Do you want each player to have a more-or-less equal shot, or do you want to force expansion by giving the starting positions only one piece of the resource puzzle? In either case, be sure to scatter a number of random resources about, in a fairly equitable fashion; unless you can calculate the exact number of resources you want out there, it's better to err on the side of too much than too little.

Remember that variety is as important as quantity: you need all types to build the full range of units and structures in the game. The opposite is true with artifacts, where your game won't suffer too much from their paucity but will suffer if there are too many fizbot wands floating about. And keep in mind that to recruit the best monsters, you have to have plenty of resources floating about to build their homes.

The Dragons guard the entrances.

As for towns and castles, it all depends on your goal. Longer games and larger maps need more castles to produce the numbers of units necessary to conquer the world. Smaller or shorter games can get away with fewer castles; the little scenario example here only has four, one per hero. In most cases this should insure a short, intense conflict, but it is also possible that one or more heroes will have bad luck and take extra long to develop. No matter what you do, be sparing with towns and castles. Keep them relatively rare and valuable, or watch your scenario degenerate into a battle of production. Of course if that's what you want. . . .

Here's how to protect an artifact: recruit your neighborhood hydra to stand watch.

In the case of the scenario example for this chapter, the results are pretty much as expected. A period of time building up, basic monsters, and a short, brutal fight to the end. You can of course develop much more elaborate games, blending more and more might and magic into your personal fantasy creation. That's the beauty of a good editor.

Space Bucks

pace Bucks provides a complex simulation without bogging the gamer down in needless minutia, yet managing the myriad production facilities, spacecraft, and commodities can bewilder even the most astute cyber executive—not to mention us. Nevertheless, after numerous hours of producing Ambrosia and green dogs, here are some tips that may help you bury those Tesarians under a mound of money.

LAUNDRY LISTS

First off, let's go through a list of hints that are useful throughout the game. Then we will discuss some general strategies.

PLANETS AND STARPORTS

Rule numero uno: don't pay too much for landing rights. If the degree of difficulty is set at beginner, propose no more than half of the initial offer. This should do the trick unless another race attempts to underbid you.

Once the starport is yours, the key to milking every possible buck from the planet is development. But wait! Move that cursor away from the "Build Luxury" button. True, a restaurant or stadium will raise the consumer satisfaction index, yet so will consistently supplying the inhabitants' needs—and it won't cost you nearly as much. The goal for each planet's growth should be starting an

CD-ROM
Check out the CD-ROM included in this book for the demo version of *Space Bucks*.

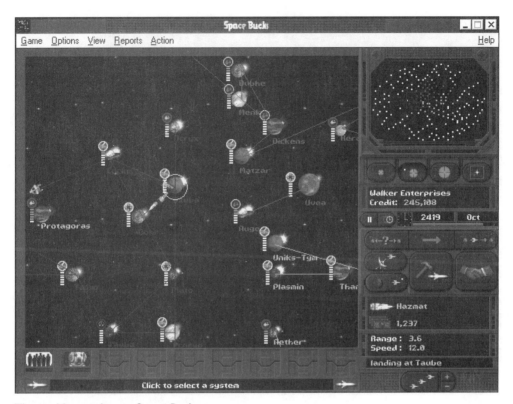

The world according to *Space Bucks*.

appropriate industry and raising the development level to at least four—the plane that allows specialized goods to be produced.

The best way to raise a planet's development level is traffic. Early in the game, develop a *hub* system of three or four planets and set up a couple of routes incorporating all the spheres of the system. This will give a lot of business to each starport and rapidly increase its growth.

Before leaving the celestial bodies, here is a couple of words on picking the right planet for the job. Glenn Oliver, *Space Buck*'s production engineer, believes the type of planets initially chosen for development and their proximity to suitable trading partners is the most important facet of the game. Ideally, this *hub* will include divergent types of worlds (needed for diverse raw materials) and different races (needed to effectively trade specialty goods).

Choose a variety of worlds and races to populate your hub.

SHIP SHAPE

Planets and their attendant starports are only one part of the equation. You may own all the launchpads in the galaxy, but without a properly configured, efficient fleet you won't get very far—literally. When choosing and subsequently utilizing a fleet the by-word, as with all else in the game, is *optimization*. Ensure the flying stock is configured to your needs. Frequently this means building custom ships. In the early stages of development, not many types of ships are offered. However, if you build a custom ship, you can attend to those short distance, high volume cargo runs more efficiently.

Speaking of efficiency, don't let ships travel empty—usually. The "delay until full" button on the configure cargo screen is a powerful tool. By clicking this icon those big cargo ships will wait at the starport until their bellies are full, rather than loading what is currently available then blasting off. A word of caution: it is a good idea to examine

Name	Drive	Weapon	Shield	Speed	Range	Status	Profit/Route
Antlia	1			5.4	2.8	landing at Dzuba	13,187
Big Far Reach	3	4	4	10.8 W	4.5	unloading at Dzuba	29,298
Explorer	2	1	2	12.0	3.6	moving to Tasso	24,336
Hazmat	2	1	2	12.0	3.6	moving to Taube	9,295
Northern Adv Goods	1	2	2	5.4	2.8	moving to Dzuba	12,363
Number 2	1			5.4	2.8	moving to Bohr	21,022
Persimmon	2	3	4	8.4	3.6	Wait at Calaeno	18,605
Southern Arms Ship	1	2	2	6.0	2.8	moving to Brahe	11,027
Walker Enterprises	1			6.0	2.8	moving to Dzuba	11,005
Western	2	1	2	10.8	3.6	Wait at Ancha	11,586

The Fleet

a route's profit closely (using the view menu) after engaging the wait option. Sometimes the profit you gain from a full cargo bay on a particular leg of a trade route will be lost due to the overall reduction in volume (due to a longer interval between runs) for the entire circuit.

UPGRADES

As the game progresses, the man from IGN will report numerous advances in space flight technology. From better shields to more powerful weapons, technology marches on. Supplying your ships with these upgrades can get costly, especially when equipping a large fleet. The solution is simple—don't do it. At least avoid upgrading all ships. Pirates have a tendency to target the larger vessels that are carrying the more valuable cargo. Spend money to give these platforms the latest in weapon technology and leave the older, smaller shuttles to their own devices. On the other hand, Glenn Oliver claims the amount of ransom the pirates demand depends on how easily they feel they may defeat the targeted ship in combat. In other words, Pirates will demand less ransom from merchants packing the latest in weapon technology than from cargo ships with last year's defense systems.

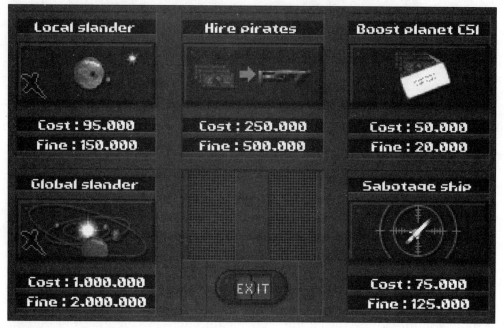

Shopping for upgrades

CONFIGURATION

Every ship in the fleet should be configured for every stop—no ifs, ands, or buts. Although at first glance this may seem like a daunting task, it isn't hard if you configure each ship when built. When configuring cargo holds, ensure each planet is getting what it needs. If a cargo is highlighted in red on the planet screen, the gamer has an unfulfilled obligation to provide the item to the planet in question. Make sure there are no hidden obstacles blocking the item's receipt.

In a recent game, we configured a cargo liner to carry green dogs to a Secanii starport. The liner was to pick up hazardous waste (necessary to make the emerald pups), deliver it to the Tesarians, wait until a unit of green dogs was turned out, and transport them to the Secanii. Unfortunately, once portside at the Tesarian planet, the ship just sat there—nothing happened. On further investigation the reason was discovered: at their current level of development the Tesarians required five toxics to make a brood (or whatever) of exotic animals. With orders to wait until full and not enough toxics available to make the product, the ship was useless. Once the hold order was rescinded the ship continued on its route, bringing additional toxics to the Tesarians, who in turn

Your Average Starport

were able to breed the Secanii's much treasured exotic animals. The lesson learned? You must constantly monitor cargo ship configuration to assure the goods are getting where you want them.

Finally, name your ships appropriately. If there is a vessel used exclusively to haul toxics between the southern planets in your empire, don't let the computer name it Persimone. Why not call it Toxic-South? As the fleet grows, you'll find this helps to keep straight who does what.

THE BEGINNING AND END OF IT

We've talked about starports, ships, and the cargo they carry, but how does all this fit together to make you the Donald Trump of the twenty-first century? Let's briefly take a look at a typical game and the strategies that lead to success. A *Space Bucks* contest can be divided into three parts: beginning, middle, and end (pure genius isn't it?).

In the beginning, look for a sweet deal—that hub of commerce that will fund your initial expansion into the nearby systems. Find three or four planets that provide mutually beneficial and divergent resources. If the races are good trading partners, so much the better; this, however, isn't pivotal. Once the route is established, profit is accruing, and development levels are rising, so it is time to expand. Do so rapidly, yet intelligently. Look for trading partners who will maximize the future trading of specialty goods.

As you expand operations things will get frantic, so make frequent use of the pause button. Keep an eye on the rise and fall of quarterly profits. It is possible to glance at the company display, note the income accumulating and believe all is well. Unfortunately as you glance away, the quarterly bills may come due, showing in truth what is a somewhat bleaker picture.

Now the mid game. This time should be devoted to obtaining and trading manufactured and specialty goods. Your fleet will also need to evolve. Invest in large cargo carriers, some of which will probably need extended ranges in order to bring the specialty goods to the species that want them. When there is a slight break in the action check your company's pricing and maintenance fees in the operations menu. The

Walker Enterprises	Last Quarter	This Year 2422	Last Year 2421
INCOME			
Total	65,619	48,236	265,901
EXPENSES			
Cost of Sales	4,023	2,789	16,761
Construction cost	0	0	0
Overhead	32,644	0	130,578
Total	36,667	2,789	147,338
Net Income	28,952	45,447	118,562

Last year's spreadsheet

Make sure your fleet is always evolving.

pricing index can usually be raised to 125 without affecting the consumer satisfaction index. Lower the maintenance pricing to 40.

The endgame goal is sinking the surviving competition. An effective ploy is to slander the enemy's reputation in a critical starport—ideally one your minions may use once the competition has been ousted. If the money is available, a general slander campaign can devastate all but the strongest opponents.

That's it: Now you've got a plan for how to build a trading empire to stand the test of time, and all in 1500 words. Hopefully it will work for you. If so, we'll meet at the other end of the universe where we'll contemplate our fortunes, sip Ambrosia, and rub our dog's green fur.

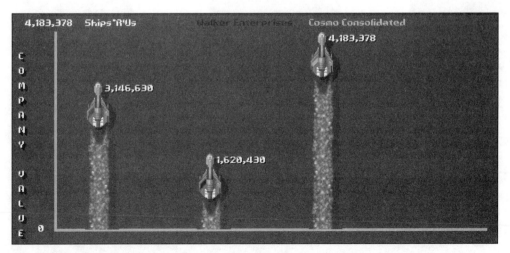

Hey, nobody wins all the time.

17

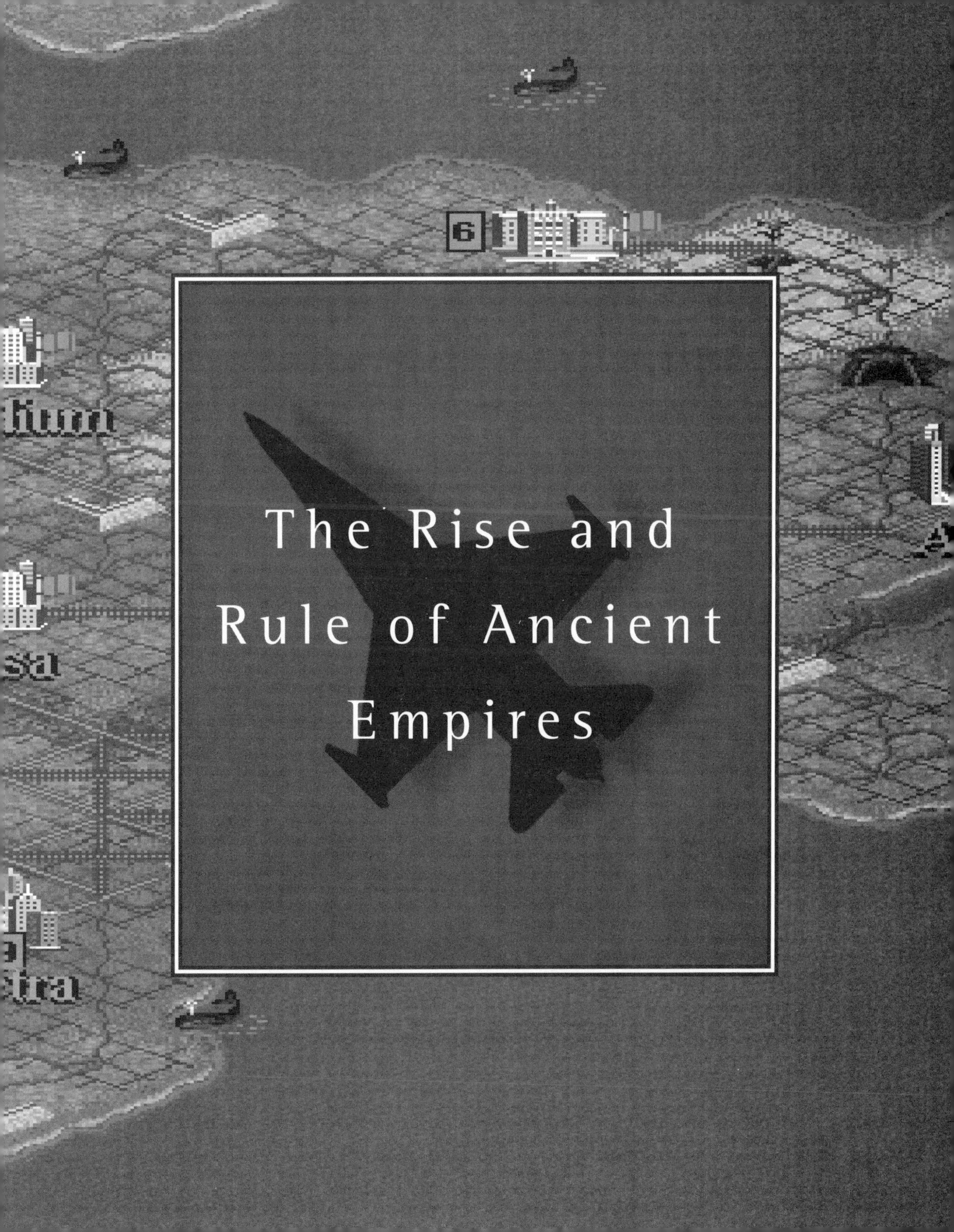

The Rise and
Rule of Ancient
Empires

Welcome to *The Rise and Rule of Ancient Empires*, otherwise known as Survival 101, final exam. You're out in the middle of the wilderness, further from civilization than a televangelist is from reality, without even the most basic modern conveniences. Your assignment has three parts. First, build a settlement and survive. Second, turn that settlement into a thriving city. Third, expand your single city into a wide-spread empire, complete with trade, education, agriculture, and mighty armies. For extra credit, take over the world. Okay, so it's not the easiest thing that anyone's ever asked you to do, but since when was global conquest supposed to be simple?

SURVIVAL OF THE FITTEST

As the game starts, your only means of taming the forbidding wilds is a single unit of settlers. They've probably been walking a long time, and they're mighty anxious to get started on this whole empire thing, so just pick a spot and they'll dig in and call it a city. The type of terrain that the little guys start out on is the type that they are best at living in, so definitely stick with that terrain for your first settlement. If it's at all possible, try to pick a spot for your settlement that has four squares of your primary terrain available on all sides, or at least

CD-ROM
Check out the CD-ROM included in this book for the demo version of *The Rise and Rule of Ancient Empires*.

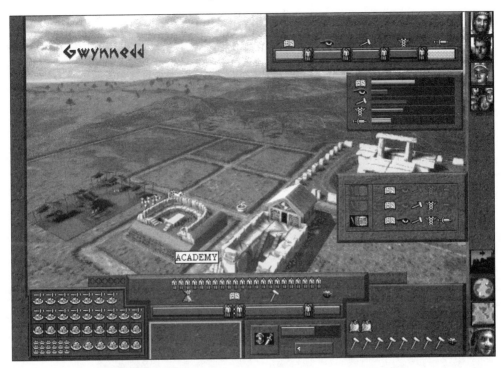

Establishing a Primary City

some kind of habitable terrain for four squares on all sides. (Habitable means anything other than an ocean. This is *Rise and Rule*, not *SimFish*.)

Once you've chosen your site, your settlers will bang together a town hall and a school and then proceed to starve if you don't get off your keister and start managing them. Go to the city view, and crank food production all the way up. Then nudge the slider bar down until your food display shows just one green "overfeeding" icon. Overfeeding is the best thing you can do for your cities, since it keeps your people happy, and healthy, and generally tends to convince them not to throw you out and go join whichever culture has managed to invent ramen noodles and the pop-tart.

Now, divide your remaining workforce between production and resource-gathering, and set them to producing a settler unit. Cycle through turns until the settler unit is complete. If, at some point, your food display shows more than one overfeeding icon, move the slider down again so that only one green icon appears, then increase production and resources accordingly.

IMPERIAL EXPANSION FOR FUN AND PROFIT

As soon as the settler unit is complete, move it four spaces away from your city and start a satellite settlement. (Cities can't be built any closer than four spaces from each other, probably due to the fact that the settlers founding the city don't want to live near their nagging in-laws, which is likely why they left their homes in the first place.) Once again, divide the new settlement's workforce between food gathering and producing another settler unit. As soon as your primary city puts the finishing touches on its next settler unit, send it four spaces away from both of your cities and start another satellite settlement.

Continue production of settlers in both of the satellite cities, until each one has produced two or three settler units each. Use three of these to start additional satellite settlements. (Placing satellite towns in a star pattern around you primary city is preferable because it simplifies trading and incidentally makes you look like you have some sort of plan.)

This graphic shows you how to arrange satellite cities in a star pattern around your primary city.

Send the other settlers to nearby areas, preferably with varied terrain, to start additional settlements. We'll call these production cities, because they're going to be producing the bulk of your armies later in the game.

Once your primary city finishes cranking out that second settler unit, don't just let it sit around idle. After all, you never know what your little citizens might get up to if you don't give them something to do 24 hours a day. Hey, you'll never be a good militaristic despot until you learn the art of mandatory industry! In this case, it's time for your primary city to get into architecture: city edifices, public structures, you know . . . buildings. And whenever you start producing buildings in a city, your first priority should be to build the second level of your town hall. Why? You want to build the second level of town hall because it will automatically monitor your food production and prevent your city from running out of victuals and having to eat its politicians. Once you've finished with that level, start work on a market.

THE OLD COLLEGE TRY

Now that all five of your satellite cities have been established, and have generated some settlers to start production cities, set them each to producing light infantry. As each unit is complete, set it to exploring. The more terrain you explore, the more warning you'll have of an approaching enemy, so build about three or four scouting units per city and send them on their way. Once these are done, it's time to convert your satellite cities to college towns. Stop production completely in all five cities, and reassign the production and resource-gathering workforce to studying. In each of the cities, choose a single one of the five skills that you can learn, and study only that one skill. It will advance rapidly in only a few turns.

Remember those production cities you were going to found? As soon as you start each city, set it to building troops to patrol the area or settlers to start even more production cities. (The more cities you have, the bigger your empire will get, and the bigger your empire gets, the less people will dare to call you a megalomaniac.) If the unit that your city is trying to produce can't quite be built in a single turn, reduce the resources and production allocated to it so that it has just enough to be finished in two turns. (Hey, if it's going to take two turns anyway, you'd might as well use the extra manpower for overfeeding or study!)

Keep an eye on the morale level and your popularity level in all the cities you've built so far. If either level drops precipitously, you'll have to do something superficially nice to make the people think that you have their best interests at heart. Stop troop production or learning in the affected city, increase food gathering, and produce a

A satellite city is converted to a college town.

building. Extra food and new buildings may not be as cool as monogrammed T-shirts or a week-long holiday in honor of the wombat god, but they will increase morale and popularity. Once popularity is back up, you can set the city back to its assigned chore and rest assured that it won't be kicking you out.

PEDDLING YOUR WARES

About this time, the market will be finished in your primary city. This will allow you to build merchants. Build five merchant units, and assign each one to go between your primary city and one of your satellite cities. (This way, if a satellite city is having trouble meeting its food needs, the merchants can transfer surplus kiwi fruit and pork shoulders from your primary city to prevent starvation.)

Next, reassign your resource gatherers and production workers to studying all five skills, until your primary city has enough knowledge to build philosophers. Build

Once the market in the primary city is complete, you can build merchant units in your satellite cities.

five philosopher units, and group each one with one of the merchants. This way, the skill being learned in each satellite city will be transferred to the primary city, without the primary city having to do any additional research. (Hey, if you could find a way to trade pork shoulders for the ability to do calculus without having to study, you'd do it too!) Once the philosophers

> **NOTE**
>
> These tips were written to work with the patched version of *Rise and Rule*. The strategies are different than the ones that you would use with the non-patched version. However, since the patch adds a considerable level of variety, cunning, and ferocity to the opposing AI cultures, any Real Gamer who's heard of the patch is obviously already using it. If you haven't heard of the patch, you have now, and you'd probably better download it quickly, to save yourself the jeers of your friends who already have it and are playing against tougher opponents than you are.

Production cities allow you to build light cavalry, but you'll need to build up even more military power.

are done, have the city produce new types of buildings, since this will allow the construction of better troops.

As soon as each of your satellite cities learns everything about its assigned skill, then you can set it up to produce buildings or troops. The philosopher traveling between it and your primary city will carry knowledge to it of the other four skills, and it will advance to being able to create new kinds of buildings without any further research. At this point, you're really going to need those new buildings, because the knowledge of how to build better troops is going to be vital. Your scouts have probably already encountered most, if not all, of the opposing civilizations, and you're going to need to be ready to face them. And the light infantry being cranked out by your ever-increasing number of production cities will only do you so much good if your opponents are currently cranking out missile and cavalry units!

You can now build
Heavy Missile...

Build a few of these babies, and add some cities to your empire.

THE WINDS OF WAR

Now let's look at how to turn your opponents into dust, complete with big screechy circling vultures and those nasty little carrion beetles that bury anything that looks particularly past-tense.

At this point, your primary and satellite cities should be advanced enough to create troops that don't fall down in a stiff breeze. Build a few cavalry, missile, or heavier infantry units, and send them off exploring. By now, most of your first batch of scouts will probably be dead from one thing (enemy troops) or another (more enemy troops).

A new batch of a dozen or so exploring teams, preferably with stronger-than-cardboard armor, will assist greatly in your intelligence efforts. Band two or three units together so a random encounter with a single unit of enemy scouts won't cut your explorations short.

There may not be weight limits on spandex, but there sure are on galleys.

If one of your satellite cities is on the water, you should also build a galley or three, load them with troops, and send them scouting, since this is the only way you can explore the wide water areas. Keep in mind, however, that galleys do have weight limits, and if you load more than two units on a light galley or four on a heavy galley, you run the risk of shipwreck.

This is also a good time to crank out a few more philosophers. Because your production cities are busy making infantry and settler units instead of learning, the only way that they're ever going to advance is if you bring knowledge in from your advanced cities (think of it as sort of a bronze-age bookmobile program). The best way to handle it is to assign a philosopher group to travel between one of the advanced cities and a production city, then another philosopher group to travel between that production city and the one next to it, and so on. This will transfer skills throughout your empire, and give every production city the chance to build the kind of cool stuff that your more advanced cities are showing off.

Use the fine art of preaching peace while practicing war.

READY TO MEET THE WORLD

Just about the time your cities are starting to turn into the advanced centers of trade and learning you've always dreamed of, you can pretty much guarantee your opponents' scouts will finally get a little too close to your empire. This means it's time to decide whether to be a nice-guy diplomat or a Rambo-esque kill-'em-all warmonger. It's probably best to stay away from the completely xenophobic attitude. You'll find that the act-real-friendly-then-stab-'em-in-the-back-and-take-their-cities approach works much better. As soon as one of your scouts encounters an opponent for the first time, start sending messages of greetings and peace. And keep sending them every few turns, since repetition seems to reinforce your diplomatic efforts considerably.

Hey, it doesn't *always* work; sometimes they'll go right ahead and declare war on you because they don't like your shirt, or because your empire invented the leather saddle first while they're still getting butt-blisters from horse blankets. But when it does work, it buys you time to put your little plan of friendliness and betrayal into action.

You'll find that there are really only two ways to deal with an enemy city. You can use overwhelming force to go in and raze it to the ground, which is probably the most fun in the short run. Or you can make yourself more popular than the city's current leader, then saunter in with a few troops and "liberate the people from their current oppressive dictatorial regime." You may prefer the latter course, since adding an enemy city to your own empire means that you get a fully functioning, stable settlement, in your enemy's territory, capable of cranking out troops from the moment you take it over. And there's really only one way to make yourself more popular to the denizens of a particular city than the guy who actually founded the place. It's the same way you make yourself popular to your own people: overfeed them and teach them new skills. For that, you'll need to set up a trade route for merchants and philosophers.

BLAZING A TRAIL

If you plan to trade with an opponent's city, you may want to build a few production cities between your empire and his. Send troops along to protect your settlers. As you establish each new city, pump up its size by adding those troops to the city's population. In city view, click on the little graphic of each troop unit, drag it to the city's population display, and drop it off. Each troop unit reassigned in this manner will add 100 people to the city's population. With these settlements in place, your units traveling towards enemy territory will have a place to re-supply, less of a chance of starving, and, for many of them, the last mug of ale they'll ever quaff.

Next, make several troop/merchant/philosopher groups, and send one to each new settlement. Once they're all in place, assign each team go between its city and the previous city, transferring goods and information down the line from your advanced cities. Once the skill level in the new settlements starts to rise, send additional teams to the cities near the end of the line. Assign each team to go between one of the new cities and an enemy city. This will raise your popularity with your enemy's population, and the troops should keep your merchant/philosopher teams from being killed by the first unit of enemy light infantry that happens to take offense at the fact that you're gaining popularity.

Okay, so now you're ready to kick a little bit of Mesopotamian keister, or Celtic backside, or whatever it is that you feel like kicking. The old clichés of overwhelming force and safety in numbers are just as applicable in ancient warfare as they are on the streets of LA today. No matter how you look at it, a maxed-out group of heavy cavalry units or heavy infantry can waltz in and just request the keys to an opponent's city, or wipe out a lesser grouping of troops with little more effort than a backhand slap

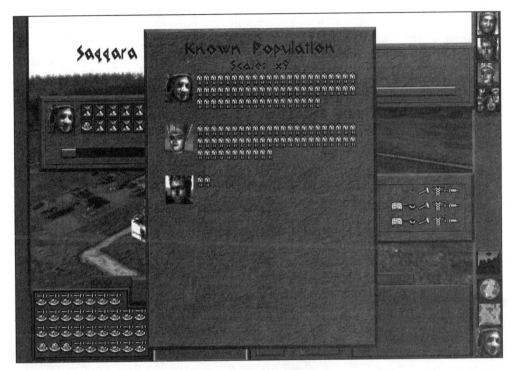

That old axiom "there's safety in numbers" is applicable here.

and an evil grin. Sound like a piece of cake? Wrong. One of the first things you'll find about moving large numbers of troops around is that they're about as slow as a three-toed tree sloth on a hot summer day. So if you want to get a massive army somewhere in a hurry, you'll do better to move it there in pieces. Send the units individually to a location near where you plan to attack, and then group them there.

MOVE 'EM OUT!

Something to keep your eye out for when moving large numbers of individual units is a situation called *clumping*. Clumping is when a unit heading one direction hits the end of its movement allowance right on top of a unit which hasn't moved yet. This joins them into a group, and the fresh unit's movement allowance is wasted, since the other group can't move with it. Fortunately, you can separate any units that you don't want grouped, as long as the unit you want to un-group still has at least one space of movement allowance left. Click on the army graphic on the map to bring up the army

display, then click on the unit icon for the unit you want to move out of the group. Click on a nearby spot within that unit's movement allowance, and it'll go there.

Another fun trick for moving troops quickly from one place to another can be used if there's a large body of water between your territory and your enemy's. Since troops and galleys have separate movement allowances, you can actually set up a system of ferries to pick up troops on one side of the water, take them across (using the grouping/un-grouping trick to relay them from galley to galley if the water is too wide for a single ship's movement allowance), then unload them on the other side, usually with troop movement allowance to spare. Cheating? Good heavens, no! If the game allows you to do it without hacking into the code, that's not cheating, is it?

Once all your units are in position, you can group them into massive armies and go lay waste to the enemy! If his people particularly like you, then you can just take over his cities and use them to create backup troops. If you didn't manage to get merchant/philosopher teams to an enemy city, or if your popularity there wasn't high

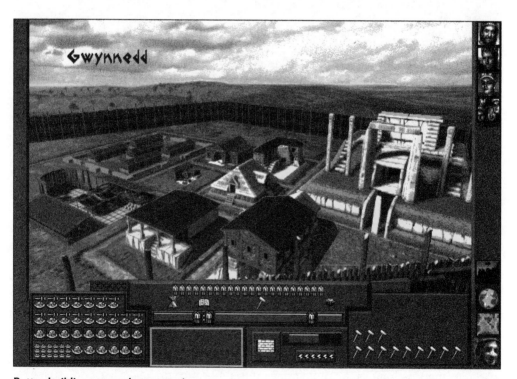

Better buildings mean better armies.

enough, then camp a big ol' army next to his city to starve the people out and cause your enemy's popularity to plummet, or else just keep sending in troops until the city is completely destroyed. In this case, the old childish attitude of "if I can't have it, nobody can," actually works in your favor. After all, cities might be able to produce troops to oppose you, but ruins definitely will not.

Good luck to you, and may your empire flourish!

CONGRATULATIONS! You have purchased a 6-issue subscription to COMPUTER GAMES Strategy Plus magazine. Plus, you have received a great COMPUTER GAMES Strategy Plus book with a CD-ROM. Send no money—your subscription is already paid. To activate your subscription, simply tear out this form, fill it out, fold, seal, stamp, and mail it. Current subscriptions will be extended. (Source 31002)

NAME _____

STREET _____ Apt _____

CITY _____

STATE _____ ZIP _____

E-MAIL ADDRESS _____

TELEPHONE (_____) _____

This form is proof-of-purchase for a 6-issue subscription to COMPUTER GAMES Strategy Plus magazine. Subscription price $19.99 (U.S.). Subscription must be activated by September 1, 1997.

This offer valid only for residents of the United States.

FOLD HERE AND SEAL

COMPUTER GAMES Strategy Plus
P.O.Box 3000
Danville, NJ 07834

THE PLAYABLE GAME DEMOS INCLUDED ON THE CD ARE:

Close Combat
Command and Conquer
Mission Force: Cyberstorm
Warcraft II
Battleground: Shiloh
Caesar II
Battleground: Gettysburg
Battleground: Waterloo
AfterLife
Allied General
Battle Isle 2220
Heroes of Might and Magic
Rise and Fall of Ancient Empires
Space Bucks
Steel Panthers
Settlers II
Conquest of the New World
Fantasy General

This CD has an autoplay feature for all gamers using Windows 95 and NT. Simply insert the CD and it will start automatically.

If you are a Windows 3.1 gamer, follow these instructions to install the easy-to-use interface that will let you browse and install the CD's contents:

1. In Program Manager, select the Run command from the File menu.

2. In the Run window, type D:\INSTALL and then press Enter. If your CD-ROM drive is not your D drive, replace D with the correct letter.

3. The Installer will create an icon in Program Manager for Interactive Entertainment's point-and-click program. This program will assist you when installing the games from the CD-ROM to your hard drive.

To see information or install individual games, highlight the game name in the right panel and then click the appropriate button.